A Woman of Prayer

BETTY HENDERSON

journeyforth®

Greenville, South Carolina

Cover image by Veer, Inc.

The fact that materials produced by other publishers may be referred to in this volume does not constitute an endorsement of the content or theological position of materials produced by such publishers.

All Scripture is quoted from the Authorized King James Version.

Amy Carmichael, "For Our Children." CLC Publications. Used by permission.

Ron Hamilton, *Faithful Men*, *verse 2*, lyrics only © 1995 by Majesty Music, Inc. All rights reserved.

Herbert Lockyer Jr., *All the Prayers of the Bible*. Taken from **All the Prayers of the Bible** by HERBERT LOCKYER JR. Copyright © 1959, 1987 by Zondervan Publishing House. Used by permission of The Zondervan Corporation.

William M. Runyan, "Lord, I Have Shut the Door." © 1923. Ren. 1951 Hope Publishing, Co., Carol Stream, IL 60188. All rights reserved. Used by permission.

A Woman of Prayer

Betty Henderson

Design by Jamie Miller
Composition by Melissa Matos

© 2006 BJU Press
Greenville, South Carolina 29609
JourneyForth Books is a division of BJU Press.

Printed in the United States of America

ISBN 978-1-59166-693-6

15 14 13 12 11 10 9 8 7 6

With loving gratitude I dedicate this book to the women of the Wednesday morning Ladies Bible Study at Colonial Hills Baptist Church in Indianapolis, Indiana. Your faithful attendance, your love for our Lord, and your biblical responses to the study of God's Word are a great blessing and encouragement to this teacher.

A special word of thanks is due my husband, Joe. For thirty-five years he has been my continual example of godly living, my encourager, and my faithful partner in the work of God.

O teach me, Lord, that I may teach
The precious things Thou dost impart;
And wing my words that they may reach
The hidden depths of many a heart.

—Frances Havergal

CONTENTS

CHAPTER ONE
An Introduction to Prayer

"One of his disciples said unto him, Lord, teach us to pray." (Luke 11:1)

A good place to begin any study of prayer is to look at the prayer life of our Lord. We know that Jesus Christ is our great example for righteous living in every area of His life, and this is especially true regarding His prayer life. The disciples often observed Him as He sought His Father's face. They realized from watching Him that a time alone with God was not a priority in their own lives. So one day they came to Jesus with the request we find in Luke 11:1. It's a needful request for all believers, isn't it? Perhaps we need to join the prayerless disciples in their earnest request, "Lord, teach *me* to pray!"

1. What is your definition of prayer? _____

_____

_____

_____

2. Why do you think prayer is so important in a believer's life? _____

_____

_____

_____

3. Do you agree or disagree with the following statement? Why?

"Prayer is the greatest activity of service that the Christian can render."[1]

_____

_____

Do you know believers who have ministries of prayer? Why are there so few who consider this to be a ministry? _____

_____

_____

_____

The Savior's Example

4. Our Lord had a great ministry of prayer. He also gave frequent instruction regarding the importance of speaking to our heavenly Father. Read the following Scriptures for examples of when He prayed and answer the following questions:

Matthew 26:36–46

Where? _____

Who was present? _____

Matthew 27:46

Where? _____

Mark 1:35

When? _____

Where? _____

Luke 6:12

When? _____

Luke 9:28–30

On what occasion? _____

Who was present? _____

John 11:41–44

On what occasion? _____

The Savior's Exhortations

Jesus not only taught by example but also taught by His words. Many of those words had to do with prayer. Read each verse below, and then answer the questions.

5. **Matthew 6:5–8**

   What dangers does Jesus warn of in verses 5 and 7? _____

   _____

   _____

   What warning and promise does He give in verse 8? _____

   _____

   _____

6. **Matthew 7:7–11**

   What great promises do we find here? _____

   _____

   _____

Luke records the great model upon which to fashion our prayers. It is from the mouth of our Lord, and the pattern still applies to twenty-first-century Christians.

7. **Luke 11:2–4**

   What are the first three requests in this "Disciple's Prayer"?

   _____

   _____

   _____

   What are the next four requests? (Note that daily bread is not mentioned as the first request.)

   _____

   _____

   _____

   _____

   What is the closing doxology (praise)? (See Matthew 6:13 also.)

   _____

   _____

8. **John 14:13–14**

What requirement for answered prayer is given twice in these verses? What does this mean?

_____

_____

_____

_____

9. **John 15:7**

What additional requirement for answered prayer do we find in this verse? How does a believer meet this requirement?

_____

_____

_____

_____

The Servant's Eagerness

On at least one occasion, the disciples expressed an eagerness about learning to pray. We find several other instances, however, in which they preferred their own wisdom or power, or chose sleeping instead of praying.

> _To be little with God in prayer is to be little for God in service._
> AUTHOR UNKNOWN

10. **Mark 9:28–29**

What question do the powerless disciples have for Christ?

_____

_____

What is Jesus' answer, and what does this mean?

_____

_____

_____

Why are present-day believers often as powerless as these early apostles?

_____

_____

11. Read Luke 11:1–4 and answer the following questions:

    What was Jesus doing when He was approached about the subject of prayer? _____

    _____

    What was the request made by the disciples, and how did Jesus answer them? _____

    _____

    _____

    _____

It is interesting to note what these men did *not* request. They did not ask, "Lord, teach us a prayer." Nor did they ask, "Lord, teach us to preach." Their request was not even, "Lord, teach us to serve." Their heart burden was to know how to be faithful in prayer. Did they ever become prayer warriors? A careful reading of the book of Acts will reveal the answer!

When is the last time you made this same request to our Lord?

_____

When I pray for my own ministry needs, I have found this request, along with the one found in Luke 17:5, to be very needful in my life.

> *Let us go alone in secret,*
> *And unburden all our care*
> *At the feet of our Redeemer,*
> *In the simple, earnest prayer.*
> FANNY CROSBY

The Savior's Entreaties for Us

There is great comfort for our hearts in the truth that Christ our Redeemer is at the right hand of the Father interceding for us. Before we close this lesson on the prayer life of our Savior, let's look briefly at this great truth.

12. Using a dictionary, define *intercessor*.

    _____

    _____

13. The Savior interceded for many while on earth. Read the following verses to find examples of His intercession.

    Luke 22:31–32

    For whom did He pray? _____

    What was His specific request? _____

    Luke 23:34

    For whom did He pray? _____

    What was the occasion? _____

    John 17:8–9, 20

    For whom did He pray? _____

14. According to Romans 8:34, where is Christ now and what is He doing?

    _____

    _____

15. The book of Hebrews has much to say about our interceding High Priest. In Hebrews 7:24–25, what three things do we learn about Him?

    _____

    _____

    _____

    Why should these truths bring comfort to our hearts? _____

    _____

    _____

> *He ever lives above,*
> *For me to intercede;*
> *His all-redeeming love,*
> *His precious blood to plead;*
> *His blood atoned for all our race,*
> *His blood atoned for all our race,*
> *And sprinkles now the throne of grace.*
>
> CHARLES WESLEY

Blessed Lord, Thou canst teach me to pray. I ask Thee this day to enroll my name among those who confess that they know not how to pray as they ought, and especially I ask Thee for a course of teaching in prayer. Lead me to cast away my thoughts of what I think I know, and make me kneel before Thee in true teachableness and poverty of spirit. Lord, forgive my sin of prayerlessness. Lord, teach me to pray.[2]

Closing Thoughts

One of the greatest tragedies of a believer's life is not unanswered prayer, but unoffered prayer. Are we grieved over our sin of prayerlessness? When we look at the importance prayer played in the life of our Savior, surely we see that we are like the disciples and are in great need of enrolling in the school of prayer. May the Lord teach us to be about the business of prayer! This is my prayer as we study these lessons together.

There is little value in studying and reading about prayer if we do not pray! In fact, learning about prayer can be positively harmful because it increases our responsibility and intensifies our guilt if we fail to pray. Prayer is one of the highest privileges of the child of God, the most significant form of service that can be rendered to God and men, and is the duty of every believer. Therefore, we must pray![3]

PRAYERS FROM THE PAST

A well-known author once said he loved reading because of the joy of meeting people he had always wanted to know. It is truly a joy to open biographies of great Christians and have them open their hearts and lives to you. Through the years many of these faithful people have become my friends, and I have greatly profited from reading about their prayer habits. Their fervency in prayer, when compared with my weak efforts at it, has caused me to blush.

In this series on prayer, I want to introduce you to several of my praying friends. As we acquaint ourselves with them, we find that prayer was not something they engaged in on a casual basis. No, prayer was a priority, and a great privilege, for these godly men and women.

May these brief excerpts of people such as Rosalind Goforth and George Mueller in the following chapters encourage you to desire to know them in a greater way through the reading of their complete biographies. And perhaps their fervency will also be used of God to stir new breath into your prayer life. There is one thing all of these men and women had in common: fervent prayer lives. Perhaps we are still reading of them and their labors for God because they took time to bathe their service for Him in prayer.

CHAPTER TWO

Principle One: Pray Always

"Praying always with all prayer and supplication in the Spirit." (Ephesians 6:18)

In our first lesson we saw that our Savior prayed always. The apostle Paul, who spoke of continual prayer in his letter to the Ephesians, was also one who had a devout prayer life. Paul was the author of many commands concerning prayer, and we will look at some of his words. We will also look at a few of the numerous prayer commands found throughout the Old and New Testaments. The Bible speaks of the importance of prayer, and one truth we find often on its pages is that the child of God must be in a spirit of prayer always.

May our hearts be refreshed and convicted as we renew acquaintances with these great passages of Scriptures. And may the Holy Spirit be our teacher while we are considering the truthful condition of our own prayer life.

1. In the Bible we find both prayers of *supplication* and prayers of *intercession*. Using a dictionary, define *supplication* and give a Bible example of such a prayer. _____

   _____

   _____

   Define *intercession* and give a Bible example of this type of prayer.

   _____

   _____

   _____

Old Testament Prayer Commands

2. Second Chronicles 7:12–14 is one of the most familiar prayer passages in the Bible. After reading these verses, answer the following questions: What great king received this message from God? _____

In these verses God gives specific instructions regarding prayer. What does He say His people must do for Him to hear and answer their prayer?

_____

_____

_____

Does God still intend for His people to follow these commands? How do we know He hasn't changed His mind? _____

_____

_____

The wonderful book of Psalms contains countless commands to pray. We will look at only five in this lesson. In a future lesson on David's prayer life, we will look at more of these challenging psalms.

3. Read Psalm 37:5. What two commands are found in this verse?

_____

_____

If we obey these commands, what does God promise to do for us?

_____

_____

In the last week, how much time have you spent committing your way to the Lord? _____

What is the average amount of time you spend in prayer daily? Are you content with that amount? _____

What must change for you to spend more time alone with God?

_____

_____

4. Read Psalm 50:15. What prayer command is given here? _____

_____

"The day of trouble" is a good time to be in contact with God! What trouble, or concern, is on your heart today? _____

_____

When you bring that burden before the Lord, what does He promise to do? _____

After God lifts your burden, what are you commanded to do, and what are some ways you can obey this command? _____

_____

_____

_____

5. Read Psalm 55:22. What command and promise are given here?

_____

_____

_____

_____

Do you know someone who is carrying a heavy burden today? As you pray for that person, claim this verse. When you tell your friend you're praying, share that you are claiming the truths of Psalm 55:22 especially for him or her.

6. Read Psalm 62:8. Here we are told to trust God always. What command does David also give?_____

_____

So often we pour out our distressed hearts to everyone but God. Instead of spreading our troubles all over town, why not spread them before the Lord, as King Hezekiah did in II Kings 19:14?

7. Read Psalm 91:15. This is another precious promise for troubled souls. List the four things God promises to do for those who call upon Him.

_____

_____

_____

_____

> *A poor old Christian woman was accustomed to making marginal notes in her Bible, and she would place a "T" next to some verses, and a "P" next to others. Her pastor asked her what they meant, and she said, "Tried and proven. For I tried that promise on such and such an occasion and proved it to be absolutely true!"*
>
> CHARLES SPURGEON

New Testament Prayer Commands

Many New Testament verses on prayer will be woven throughout our future lessons. But in keeping with the theme of the believer's command to pray, let's take a special look at familiar instructions given by Jesus, Paul, and James. Most of these are well known to the majority of believers, but my prayer is that our souls will profit from considering them once again.

8. As He completes what we know as the Sermon on the Mount, Jesus speaks the familiar words found in Matthew 7:7–11. After reading these verses, answer the questions below.

   Jesus is commanding us to

   A _____

   S _____

   K _____

   What promise is found three times in verse 7?_____

   What additional words of assurance are spoken by our Lord in verse 8?

   _____

   What are some of the "good things" (verse 11) God has given you in response to your asking Him? _____

   _____

   _____

   _____

9. The apostle Paul's life was devoted to prayer. He often refers to his prayer life. As we look at the following commands, we can be sure that this great and godly man followed these instructions in his own life.

Romans 12:12

What does it mean to be "continuing instant in prayer"? _____

_____

_____

Ephesians 6:18

With all of our daily responsibilities, how can we be "praying always"?

_____

_____

_____

Colossians 4:2

What were Paul's instructions to the church at Colosse? _____

_____

_____

I Thessalonians 5:17

What is the giant truth found in this tiny verse? _____

_____

_____

> *Seven words that tell us why the average Christian is poor and powerless: Ye have not, because you ask not.*
> R. A. TORREY

One can surmise from the verses above that Paul was consumed with the importance of prayer. When we compare our prayer life to Paul's, we will no doubt cry out with the disciples, "Lord, teach *me* to pray!"

10. James is known as the follower of our Lord who was a "pillar" in the church at Jerusalem. It's a great thing when one is a "pillar" who prays! Read the following verses from the book of James to see if you think this Jerusalem "pillar's" priority was prayer.

James 1:5

What command with promise is given for us here? _____

_____

_____

James 4:2–3

Failure to ask God for our needs results in what?_____

_____

What reasons does James give for denial of our requests?_____

_____

_____

James 5:13–16

If we are afflicted (troubled, suffering), what are we to do? _____

_____

If we are sick, what should we request?_____

_____

According to verse 15, what must accompany our prayer? _____

_____

How is the prayer of a righteous person honored by God (verse 16)?

_____

_____

Closing Thoughts

The Bible is a prayer book. Beginning in early Genesis, and continuing page after page until John's Revelation, God was careful to record the prayers of faithful men and women. Most of these mighty prayer warriors never read a book on prayer or attended a prayer seminar. They just prayed. Yet today, when we are blessed with personal copies of the Bible and innumerable helps on prayer, we find ourselves often grieved by our sin of prayerlessness.

> *Before his death, an eminent Christian of another century confessed: "I wish I had prayed more. Even if I had worked less. From the bottom of my heart I wish I had prayed better."*[1]
>
> J. OSWALD SANDERS

I am burdened over my own puny prayer time, and I am burdened for believers like you who are concerned about your own failures in prayer. May these lessons cause us to pray with David, "I [will] give myself unto prayer" (Psalm 109:4).

Praying John Hyde

Imagine being so well known for your faithfulness in prayer that your friends give you a nickname having to do with prayer! Most of us will never have such an honor, but John Hyde (1865–1912) did. John was born in Carrollton, Illinois, and left the farm fields of the Midwest in 1892 to become a missionary to India. For twenty years, with only one furlough, he labored in the villages of India.

At the beginning of 1899 he was greatly burdened because he was seeing so few conversions in his ministry. This burden led him to spend more time on his knees than ever before. He soon began to wrestle with God in prayer until late at night; sometimes he spent all night before the Lord. Prayer literally became his meat and drink. God honored his fervent prayer, and in one year alone he saw over eight hundred in India saved and baptized.

A serious heart condition forced him to leave his beloved India in 1912. He returned to Carthage, Illinois, where he died a few months later. He is buried in the churchyard of the Presbyterian church in that town.

Prayer and communion with God came first in John's life. Is it any wonder that fellow missionaries gave him such a nickname as "Praying John"? May God lay on our hearts the truth that changed John's life: *"The time I spend alone with God is more important than any labor I do for God."*

You Didn't Ask, Seek, nor Knock

I got up early one morning
And rushed right into the day;
I had so much to accomplish
That I didn't take time to pray.

Problems just tumbled about me,
And heavier came each task;
"Why doesn't God help me?" I wondered;
He answered: "You didn't ask."

I wanted to see joy and beauty,
But the day toiled on, gray and bleak;

I wondered why God didn't show me;
He said: "But you didn't seek."

I tried to come into God's presence;
I used all my keys at the lock.
God gently and lovingly chided,
"My child, you didn't knock."

I woke up early this morning
And paused before entering the day;
I had so much to accomplish
That I had to take time to pray.

AUTHOR UNKNOWN

CHAPTER THREE
Principle Two: God Hears

"And this is the confidence that we have in him, that, if we ask any thing according to his will, he heareth us." (I John 5:14)

Around the world there are millions who pray faithfully every day. For most it is a ritual practiced with the hope of gaining favor with whatever god they are worshiping. Have we not all seen the throngs of men and boys falling on their faces in Muslim lands five times each day? Missionaries tell of those who carefully make their own god, placing it in a crude shrine where worshipers can bow down. Others count beads or light candles with the hope that their prayers will be heard. The sad truth is that most of these prayers are prayed to gods who have ears but cannot hear the pleas for help.

We who have trusted Christ and His shed blood for our salvation have been commanded to pray. Why are our prayers different from those mentioned above? What confidence do we have that others do not? Is it not the confidence that our great God is not hard of hearing and that He has promised us His ears are open unto our cries at all times? Praise God for the great theme in this lesson, which assures us that when "the righteous cry, the Lord heareth" (Psalm 34:17).

Gods Who Cannot Hear

1. Read Psalm 115:3–8. Describe the man-made gods pictured in these
   verses. _____

   _____

   _____

   _____

2. According to the psalmist in verse 8, what is the description of those who make and worship these masses of metal and stone?_____

_____

3. Read Isaiah 45:20. What similar description did Isaiah give of false gods and those who worship them? _____

_____

_____

_____

Our God Who Always Hears

4. God has given endless promises to His people. One of those promises is to hear the prayers of the righteous. What important truth do we find in Hebrews 10:23 about God the Promiser? _____

_____

5. All of the following verses speak of our hearing God. After reading the verses, write down each promise given. Why do you think God had the writers of Scripture include this same promise so many times?

Psalm 18:6 _____

Psalm 34:4, 6 _____

Psalm 34:15, 17_____

Psalm 55:17_____

Psalm 116:1–2 _____

Isaiah 59:1 _____

Hindrances to Hearing

William Cowper, a hymn writer of the past, once wrote of the "various hindrances we meet in coming to the Mercy Seat."

6. What are some of the obstacles that keep prayers from being answered?

Psalm 66:18 _____

Proverbs 28:13_____

Mark 11:25–26_____

James 1:6–7 _____

I Peter 3:7_____

7. God never overlooks sin in the life of His people. Can you think of a time in your life when your prayers were hindered because of sin? _____

_____

_____

8. Read Proverbs 28:13 again. If a person chooses to continue in her sin, God says she will not _____. On the other hand, what two things can she do if she would have the mercy of the Lord in her life? _____

Does God Hear the Prayer of the Unrighteous?

9. According to John 9:31, whose prayer does God not hear? _____

The word *sinner* is used here to describe a person who does not seek after God or care to have God control her life. She may have a form of godliness, as did the Pharisees, but she denies the need of God's power to rule in her life.

10. Read the words of John 9:31 once again. What people does God delight to hear? _____

As we've found earlier in this lesson, God always hears His children. But it is important to remember that God is not obligated to hear those who, by their own choices, do not belong to Him.

> *We cannot say with any confidence or certainty, "I shall not want," unless we can say with confidence and certainty, "The Lord is my Shepherd."*[1]
>
> AUTHOR UNKNOWN

11. In Luke 18:13 we read the words of a repentant heart. What is this prayer that our God always hears and never delays in answering? _____

_____

Give the date and place where you used this prayer, or one similar, to cry to God for salvation. _____

12. King Solomon wrote several times regarding the prayers of the unrighteous. Write out the verses below and then answer the questions.

Proverbs 15:8_____

_____

_____

_____

Proverbs 21:27 _____

_____

_____

_____

Using a dictionary, define *abomination.* _____

_____

_____

What sacrifices, or good deeds, do unrepentant men sometimes offer to God? _____

_____

_____

According to I Samuel 15:22–23 and Psalm 51:17, what does God desire more than man's good deeds? _____

_____

> *The kind of worship described in this proverb is no better than a bribe. How do people try to bribe God? They may go to church, tithe, or volunteer, not because of their love and devotion to God, but because they hope God will bless them in return. . . . We may be able to bribe people, but we cannot bribe God.*[2]

God Hears Even Me

Earlier in this lesson we were glad to agree with the psalmist when he frequently spoke of God's faithfulness in hearing our prayers. The question we now need to ask is how often does He hear us speaking to Him in prayer? How many times in the day, or in the night seasons, does He hear our voice? How often do we take advantage of this great privilege we have to speak with our God?

13. Read the following words of David and record when God heard his voice.

Psalm 5:3 _____

Psalm 55:17 _____

Psalm 145:2 _____

How does your daily prayer life compare with David's? _____

_____

_____

_____

I Will Hear His Words

14. Read Psalm 85:8. What are the first three words of this verse?

> *I am listening, Lord, for Thee,*
> *What hast Thou to say to me?*[3]

_____

15. What is the main way we hear from God today? God often spoke to Bible men audibly. Why does He not do that today? _____

_____

_____

_____

16. How much time do you spend alone with God that He may speak to your heart?_____

Closing Thoughts

We are blessed indeed to have such a wonderful, prayer-hearing God! I hope this lesson has reminded you of this fact and that you will set aside time each day so He may hear your voice in prayer and you may hear His voice through His Word.

In times of tragedies, unsaved men will often make public declarations about praying for one another. Men who curse God one day will call upon Him for help

> *Lord, I have shut the door,*
> *Speak now the word,*
> *Which in the din and throng*
> *Could not be heard;*
> *Hushed now my inner heart,*
> *Whisper Thy will,*
> *While I have come apart,*
> *While all is still.*
>
> WILLIAM M. RUNYAN

and blessing the next day. But what is the only prayer from lost men that God promises to answer? Why do men often refuse to pray this prayer, preferring only to have their temporal needs met? The Bible teaches that God is merciful to the just and the unjust. He is not under obligation to meet the needs of those who trample His name and refuse His gift of salvation.

In Psalm 116:1–2, the psalmist writes of his love for the Lord and his communion with the Lord. I want to share this with you as a final praise to our great God, Who does indeed hear our prayers!

> *I love the Lord, because he hath heard my voice and my supplications. Because he hath inclined his ear unto me, therefore will I call upon him as long as I live.*
> *(Psalm 116:1–2)*

FRANCES RIDLEY HAVERGAL—THE PRAYING HYMN WRITER

As we close this lesson, let's take a moment to remember the prayer life of one of England's well-known hymn writers, Frances Havergal (1837–79). Born into a pastor's home near Worcester, Frances was almost fifteen when she trusted in the blood of Christ and was born again.

As she grew to adulthood, she began to hunger and thirst more and more for His righteousness. She began to memorize His Word and to study it faithfully every day. The overflow of her full heart resulted in many of the lovely hymns we sing today. (Can you name any of them?)

In addition to hymn writing, she served the Lord as a children's Bible teacher and as a pianist, vocalist, devotional book author, and poet. Like many Victorians, she also loved mountain climbing in Switzerland and almost fell to her death more than once! When opportunity allowed her to travel in Europe, she was faithful to distribute tracts and witness for her Lord.

Frances felt her most important ministry was prayer. She carefully organized her prayer list so that she would not forget to bring any of her numerous friends and ministries before the throne of grace. She was especially burdened for her nephews and nieces, as well as the many children she taught in Bible classes.

By the age of forty, she was almost an invalid. Many of her ministries were no longer possible, except for the one that was most important: prayer. From her bed she served God day after day by praying for His work and His workers. At the young age of forty-two she died in Swansea, Wales. We thank our Lord for this faithful prayer servant. Her ministry continues to bless and encourage present-day believers through the singing of her hymns, such as "Like a River Glorious," "I Gave My Life for Thee," "Take My Life and Let It Be," "Who Is on the Lord's Side?" and many others.

CHAPTER FOUR

Principle Three: God Answers

"Call unto me, and I will answer thee, and shew thee great and mighty things, which thou knowest not." (Jeremiah 33:3)

In our previous two lessons we have considered these basic prayer principles:

We are to *pray always.*

God hears our prayers.

In this lesson we will study principle three, which is that *God answers* our prayers. We have His promises that this is true, and believers throughout the ages rise up to testify that it is so. In His Word, God Himself has given us countless proofs of His faithfulness in answering prayer. Can we not also join Abraham, David, Jeremiah, Hannah, Joshua, Paul, and Peter in giving testimony to His greatness in this matter?

Thousands of years ago the golden words of Jeremiah 33:3 were given to a heartbroken prophet. Down through the centuries, these words have become priceless to God's people, many of whom were also heartbroken. Someone has rightfully said that each of the words in this verse is pure gold. Gladly would believers of all centuries heartily agree.

In this lesson we're especially interested in these four golden words: *"I will answer thee."* Prepare your heart for a blessing as we study these words.

Our Golden Text

After reading Jeremiah 33:1–3, answer the following questions.

1. Where was Jeremiah when he wrote these golden words? _____

_____

2. In verse 2, how does Jeremiah describe his God? _____

_____

_____

3. What invitation does this mighty God give to His people in verse 3?

_____

_____

_____

What is the similar invitation He gives in Jeremiah 29:12–13? _____

_____

_____

_____

4. What two golden promises are given for us in Jeremiah 33:3?

_____

_____

Replace the "thee's" in this verse with your own name. Suddenly it becomes even more golden, does it not? But wait. In the Scriptures we have many more priceless promises that tell us He answers prayer. He has scattered them like gold dust throughout His precious book, and those who daily dig in His gold mine will have treasures indeed!

> *God's own people needing a command to pray? Why is this? Because, dear friends, we are very subject to fits of worldliness, if indeed that is not our usual state.*[1]
> CHARLES SPURGEON

Our Golden Promises

5. Read each of the following verses and write down the promises regarding answered prayer.

Psalm 50:15 _____

Psalm 86:7 _____

Psalm 91:15 _____

Psalm 138:3 _____

Isaiah 58:9 _____

Isaiah 65:24 _____

6. After looking over your current prayer list, ask God to direct you to the persons who would be encouraged by one of the above promises. Who are the folks you will take time to share one of the golden verses with this week? Write out their names. _____

_____

_____

> _Will He give the invitation to us to seek His face, and when we summon courage enough to fly to His bosom, will He be unjust and ungracious enough to forget to hear our cry and to answer us? Let us not think so unkindly of our God._[2]
> CHARLES SPURGEON

Our Golden Examples

As we have seen, God promised to show great and mighty things to those who call upon Him. The Scriptures are full of examples that show His power to do more than we can ask or think. Look up the following Scriptures, and after reading them, write down the request and how God answered. All of these are somewhat unusual requests, as you will see.

7. **Genesis 18:22–33**

Abraham's request was _____

_____

_____

_____

God's answer was _____

_____

_____

_____

8. **Genesis 24:3–27**

   Eliezer's request was _____

   _____

   _____

   _____

   God's answer was _____

   _____

   _____

   _____

9. **Joshua 10:12–14**

   Joshua's prayer was _____

   _____

   _____

   _____

   God's answer was _____

   _____

   _____

   _____

10. **Judges 16:23–31**

    Samson's request was _____

    _____

    _____

    _____

    God's answer was _____

    _____

    _____

    _____

11. **Jonah 2:1–9**

    Jonah's request was _____

    _____

    _____

God's answer was _____

_____

_____

_____

These men exercised the prayer principle of calling unto God, and God proved the principle we are considering today: He answers prayer. Our requests may not be as unusual as those above, but God is faithful to fulfill even the simplest burden that is on our heart.

12. What is one unusual request you have brought before His throne? How did God answer? _____

_____

_____

_____

Our Golden Opportunities

Does God always say yes to the requests we bring before Him? Most of the Bible examples we have considered involve affirmative answers. Are there not other times in the Bible when God has answered differently? In this last section of the lesson, we will consider the three answers God may give to our prayers: *yes, no,* or *wait.*

13. God's answer may be yes.

Matthew 14:28–30

Request: _____

Specific answer: _____

Acts 28:8–9

Request: _____

Specific answer: _____

> *Jesus answered. He said, "No."*
> *—Isn't no an answer?*[3]
> AMY CARMICHAEL

14. His answer may be no.

    Deuteronomy 3:23–26

    Request: _____

    Specific answer: _____

    II Samuel 12:16–18

    Request: _____

    Specific answer: _____

    I Kings 19:4

    Request: _____

    Specific answer: _____

    II Corinthians 12:7–9

    Request: _____

    Specific answer: _____

15. His answer may be wait.

    Genesis 15:2–5

    Request: _____

    Specific answer: _____

    John 11:1–7, 20–44

    Request: _____

    Specific answer: _____

    We are always glad to give a "Praise the Lord!" for a yes. What are some of the no or wait answers you have praised Him for? _____

    _____

    _____

    _____

> *He answered prayer—not in the way I sought*
> *Nor in the way that I had thought He ought;*
> *But in His own good way; and I could see*
> *He answered in the fashion best for me.*[4]
> HERBERT LOCKYER

Closing Thoughts

These three basic principles of prayer that we have considered are so very important if our prayer life is to be pleasing to God. Let's review the three once again.

Principle One: Pray _____

Principle Two: God _____

Principle Three: God _____

We have completed the fourth lesson in this series on the priority of prayer. My question for each of us is this: Has prayer become more of an understood necessity in our lives? It is not enough just to talk and read about prayer if such talking and reading do not result in increased prayer! May God so burden our heart.

Many of you have read the little book *How I Know God Answers Prayer* by missionary Rosalind Goforth. In this heart-warming book, Mrs. Goforth gives personal testimony of God's faithfulness in answering prayer for all the years she and her family served God in China. Here is a poem she wrote about her prayer adventures.

> *He answered prayer: so sweetly that I stand*
> *Amid the blessing of his wondrous hand*
> *And marvel at the miracle I see,*
> *The favours that his love hath wrought for me.*
> *Pray on for the impossible, and dare*
> *Upon thy banner this brave motto bear,*
> *   "My father answers prayer."[5]*
> ROSALIND GOFORTH

ROSALIND GOFORTH—PRAYING WIFE AND MOTHER

Rosalind Goforth (1864–1942) and her husband, Jonathan, labored as pioneer missionaries in China. Hudson Taylor, with whom they labored, gave them godly advice when they were fresh on the mission field from their native Canada. He had learned, and encouraged them to learn, that the only way to go forward in their ministry was to do so on their knees. Mrs. Goforth, in her later writings, humbly acknowledged how slowly she was to learn this truth and that most often had to learn it the hard way.

The Goforths arrived in China in the early months of 1888; they served there until 1935. Rosalind wrote six books about those years, and in one of these, *How I Know God Answers Prayer*, she relates how she learned the great but simple truth that our God is always faithful to hear and answer prayer. In her book she gives stirring personal testimonies of God's faithfulness. She always marveled at God's provision of finances and housing, physical healing for her husband and children, sustaining grace and comfort in the death of five of their eleven children, safety in the midst of civil wars, provision of needed clothing for her large family, and protection from disease on numerous occasions.

We are indeed fortunate that most of Rosalind's books are still in print. Our generation needs to be reminded that the God Who lovingly heard and answered prayer for Mrs. Goforth is the same God we serve today, and He is fully able to provide any need we have in this twenty-first century. Like her, may we keep praying for the impossible, and may we rest in her simple testimony: "My Father answers prayer."

CHAPTER FIVE

Prayer Practiced: Praying with Faith

"But without faith it is impossible to please him: for he that cometh to God must believe that he is, and that he is a rewarder of them that diligently seek him."
(Hebrews 11:6)

In Matthew 9:28, Jesus asked two needy men this question: "Believe ye that I am able to do this?" The Savior was inquiring about their faith, and this lesson is about our own faith. When we pray, do we believe God is able to perform the requests we present to Him? I was convicted recently as I read the following words from a well-known author:

> *Prayer must be in faith. Unbelieving prayer is a waste of energy, time, and words. Our Christian life began with faith, and so it must continue by faith. As a dead man is no man at all, so a prayer without faith is no prayer at all. But the prayer of faith is God's delight. Unbelief displeases God and must therefore be classified as sin.*[1]

In our last three lessons we considered a trio of important prayer principles: the command to pray always, the confidence that God hears, and the certainty that God answers. Today we have the first of three lessons dealing with the practice of prayer, and I think you will see that this lesson on praying with faith is key to all else we study in this series.

Faith Defined

    1. What is your definition of faith? _____

_____

2. What definition of faith does Paul give in Romans 4:21?_____

   _____

   _____

3. According to Hebrews 11:6, what is the only way to please God?

   _____

   _____

   This verse also teaches a great truth for all who come to God in prayer.
   What two things are we told we *must believe*? Write these below.

   _____

   _____

4. The opposite of faith is unbelief. In Genesis 3:1 we find Satan's statement
   of unbelief. It is summed up in three words. What are they?

   _____

   We must be careful that we do not harbor similar seeds of unbelief. How
   do we sometimes question God's Word?_____

   _____

   _____

> *Never think for a moment that strong faith in the Lord
> is necessarily pride. It is the reverse. It is one of the worst
> forms of pride to question the promises of God.*[2]
> CHARLES SPURGEON

Faith Displayed

There are many displays of great faith in God's Word. Who can forget
young David as he stood against Goliath or Elijah on Mt. Carmel or Daniel
and his friends as they walked by faith in Babylon or Mary as she talked with
Gabriel? But there is one Bible chapter in which God chose to display the lives
of many of His faithful men and women: Hebrews 11. Let's look again at this
wonderful record of faith in God.

5. After reading Hebrews 11:4–31, list the men and women who served God "by faith." _____

_____

_____

6. Are you surprised to find some of these people recognized as having great faith in God? Choose one and give an example of unbelief in his or her life? _____

_____

_____

_____

God is merciful, is He not? What encouragement should this give to our unfaithful hearts? _____

_____

_____

_____

7. In verse 32, God gives additional names of the faithful. Who are they?

_____

_____

_____

8. What are some of the godly works they did "through faith?" (See verses 33–35.) _____

_____

_____

_____

9. What two words in verse 33 make reference to the prayer life of these faithful ones? _____

10. The first two words of verse 36 are "and others" (KJV). Who were these "others"? Why do you think they endured such sufferings when those listed before them enjoyed triumphs? _____

_____

_____

_____

Does this mean that they had less faith or that God did not answer their prayers? _____

Give your thoughts on this. _____

_____

_____

_____

> The heroes of old, "Through faith . . .
> obtained promises," and there is no new
> way of obtaining them, my friends.
> FRANCES HAVERGAL

Our Faithful God

In writing of the attribute of the faithfulness of God, theologian Arthur Pink had these insightful words:

> Unfaithfulness is one of the most outstanding sins of these evil days. And none
> of us can claim complete immunity from this fearful sin. In how many ways
> have we been unfaithful to Christ, and to the privileges He has entrusted to us?
> How refreshing then to lift our eyes above this scene of ruin and behold One
> Who is faithful in all things, and faithful at all times. [3]

11. In the following verses, how is our God described?

Deuteronomy 7:9 _____

_____

I Corinthians 1:9 _____

_____

I Corinthians 10:13 _____

_____

Hebrews 10:23 _____

_____

Revelation 19:11 _____

_____

Without His faithfulness we have no hope! What if He could not be depended upon to do as He has promised? Great is His faithfulness to us!

12. We are not always faithful to Him, are we? What comforting promises does Paul give in II Timothy 2:13? _____

_____

_____

_____

13. According to Psalm 89:1, to whom are we to be declaring the faithfulness of God? _____

To whom, and in what ways, are you obeying this verse? _____

_____

_____

_____

"Lord, Increase My Faith!"

14. What is the request given in Luke 17:5 and who made it? _____

_____

15. The apostles' request was indeed a needy one. In Matthew 8:26 what correct assessment did Jesus make of their faith? _____

_____

Someone has said that the only little thing present in that Bible scene was their faith. There was a great storm, great fear, and a great Master. If only great faith had also been present!

16. How would Jesus describe your faith? _____

_____

_____

_____

Have you ever asked Him to increase your faith? Explain. _____

_____

_____

_____

> *O for a faith that will not shrink*
> *Though pressed by many a foe,*
> ...
> *But in the hour of grief or pain,*
> *Will lean upon its God.*
> WILLIAM BATHURST

Closing Thoughts

What shape is your faith in today? I confess that I can often be called Mrs. Little Faith, or even worse, Mrs. No Faith. How I need a daily "faith lift!" Do you surrender to the sins of unbelief and doubt as often as I do? Like the disciples, we need to come to the Lord with this simple request: "Lord, increase our faith!"

When speaking to women's groups, I have often mentioned the need of praying specific Bible requests for ourselves and others. These requests regard continued spiritual growth, and I want to share them with you. During your daily time with God, after you have sought His face regarding the burdens of your heart, ask Him to help you, and others, in these specific ways:

"Lord, teach me Thy Word." (Psalm 119:135)

"Lord, teach me to pray." (Luke 11:1)

"Lord, increase my faith." (Luke 17:5)

"Lord, keep the door of my lips." (Psalm 141:3)

"Lord, may Your beauty be upon me." (Psalm 90:17)

"Lord, establish the work of my hands today." (Psalm 90:17)

You may wish to add additional requests to the ones above, but these are often the cry of my heart as I prepare for another day.

God is able to help us change from our condition of being Mrs. Little Faith. The Lord never intended for us to remain in such a weak spiritual state. As we seek His face and walk in His ways, we will one day see our faith increased to that of Mrs. Strong in Faith (Romans 4:20). I would much rather have that epithet on my tombstone, wouldn't you?

Charles H. Spurgeon—The Praying Pastor

Charles Spurgeon (1834–92) was rightly called "The Prince of Preachers." He ministered in England, the country of his birth, all of his life. All who knew him could testify that his greatest love was Jesus Christ. His only desires were to preach the Word, reach the lost, feed the sheep, and honor His God.

Spurgeon was called to pastor a great London church at the early age of twenty. A small crowd came to hear this "boy from the country" the first time he preached in the busy city. But after hearing him, city folks began to spread the word about their new pastor, and soon the church could not hold all who came to hear God's Word preached so simply and powerfully.

What part did prayer play in the life of the great pastor of the Metropolitan Tabernacle? Dinsdale Young, a member of his congregation, often heard him pray. He gave this insight into his pastor's prayer life:

> It was memorable to hear my wonderful pastor when he preached, but it was often even more wonderful to hear him pray. Who talked with God as Spurgeon did? How naturally prayer fell from his lips. He was ever ready to pray.[4]

But the great pastor never felt his prayer life was what it should be. He once commented that he was more dissatisfied with his prayer life than anything else he did. Undoubtedly we could all say the same, could we not?

Why was C. H. Spurgeon such a great and powerful preacher? Why did thousands flock to hear him week after week? The secret of his preaching lay in his praying. He once said: "I have not preached this morning half as much as I have prayed. For every word I have spoken, I have prayed two words silently to God."[5] How different would our ministries be if we prayed like this? Are we willing to make such a sacrifice to find out?

CHAPTER SIX

Prayer Practiced: Praying with Fervency

"Let us therefore come boldly unto the throne of grace, that we may obtain mercy, and find grace to help in time of need." (Hebrews 4:16)

The practice of prayer not only involves praying with faith but also requires fervency. Have you ever heard someone pray fervently? If not, perhaps you have read of great servants of God from the past, such as Hudson Taylor, Charles Spurgeon, Amy Carmichael, or George Mueller, whose cries to God have been recorded for many generations of readers.

Of course, the Bible gives us the greatest examples of men and women who knew how to pray with fervency. We will meet only two of these. They were as different as night is from day. One was a well-known fiery Jewish prophet, the other an unknown and unnamed Gentile woman. Our merciful God heard their cries and granted them the desires of their heart. From these two lives may the Lord help us to learn the value of prayer that is fervent.

1. Using a dictionary, define the words *fervency* and *fervently* as they relate to prayer. _____

   _____

   _____

   _____

2. If a woman prays a prayer of importunity, what type of prayer is she praying? _____

3. If one is importunate in her prayer life, she (circle one)

   (a) is easily discouraged and quits.

   (b) is not discouraged by delayed answers.

   (c) is praying words from her head but not her heart.

So often our prayers are feeble or shallow. Such praying, as we will see in the next examples, secures little results and brings neither glory to God nor good to men.

The Fervent Prophet Who Cried

4. First Kings 17:1 gives us a picture of the kind of relationship Elijah had with God. Write out the phrase below: _____

   _____

5. James 5:17 speaks of this portion of I Kings when it tells us the reason Elijah was praying with such fervency. What was his specific request?

   _____

   James also tells how God answered the prophet's prayer. Write the answer below. _____

   _____

   _____

   _____

> *Think of it! The very laws of nature were suspended year after year because a God fearing man prayed.*[1]
> HERBERT LOCKYER

6. For another example of Elijah's prayer life, read I Kings 18:42–46 and James 5:18. What request did this great man now ask of God?

   _____

   Elijah prayed expecting God to answer. He kept on praying, believing God would do as He had promised. How many times did he ask God for this request? _____

   God sent a great answer to Elijah's prayer. What mighty miracle was done? _____

7. James tells us that Elijah was a man "subject to like passions as we are" (5:17). What does this mean, and why should it be an encouragement to us? _____

_____

_____

_____

8. As seen in an earlier lesson, the apostle James was a "praying pillar" in the church of Jerusalem. In James 5:16 what type of prayer does he say receives recognition from God? _____

What is the spiritual quality of the person praying? _____

James, under the direction of the Holy Spirit, said Elijah was a righteous man. Because of this, God was pleased to hear and answer his petitions for help. Would your pastor describe you as righteous? This passage in James emphasizes the need for right living before God, and fervent prayers to God, if we would have prayers that "availeth much" with God. *"The righteous cry, and the Lord heareth"* (Psalm 34:17).

The Fervent Woman Who Cried

Even as James used Elijah for an example of fervency in prayer, so Jesus used the following woman as another example. Her spirit of importunity led Jesus not only to answer her prayer but also to award her a priceless commendation. This lesson from the life of our Lord reminds us that not only great prophets can be heard in heaven!

After reading Matthew 15:21–28, answer the following questions.

9. How did this nameless woman of Canaan get Jesus' attention?

_____

What was her first request for herself, and what grievous problem was heavy on her heart? _____

_____

10. What was the unexpected response in verse 23? _____

_____

11. What expected response did the impatient disciples have to her request?

_____

_____

12. How would we have responded to the Lord's silence and the disciples' uncaring reproach? _____

Notice that this woman was not silenced by the Lord's apparent silence. Have you ever felt the heavens were silent to your cries? If so, then you will want to study the next portion of this wonderful story!

13. What other possible discouragement was dealt to her in verses 24 and 26?

_____

_____

Notice that she came even nearer to Jesus and worshiped Him. Instead of going away, what was her to-the-point reply? _____

> This dear woman did not argue with Jesus. Instead, she used Jesus' own choice of words "agreeing to be considered a dog as long as she could receive God's blessing for her daughter."[2]

14. According to verse 28, how were her fervent pleas so wonderfully rewarded, and what special commendation for her did Jesus pronounce for all to hear? _____

_____

_____

The Profitability of Our Cries

Will God still honor and answer the fervent cries of His people? The following great verses should encourage present-day women, and men, who would bring their burdens to the feet of the Savior.

> Do we pray for our children as this woman pleaded for her daughter? Have we not good reason to take her for our example?[3]
>
> CHARLES SPURGEON

15. Hebrews 4:16 is a command to pray. How are we to approach God, and what profit is promised for those who obey this command? _____

_____

_____

_____

> *Some Christians approach God meekly with heads hung, afraid to ask Him to meet their needs. Others pray flippantly with little thought. Come with reverence, for He is your King, but come with bold assurance, for He is your Friend and Counselor.*[4]

David was a powerful king with his own royal throne, but he spent continual time before God's throne of grace. Like Elijah and the Gentile woman, David fervently cried for God's help in his frequent times of distress.

16. In the following verses, write out David's pleadings and God's responses, and then rejoice and remember that these promises are for you also!

Psalm 18:6

Appeal: _____

Response: _____

Psalm 34:6

Appeal: _____

Response: _____

Psalm 55:17

Appeal: _____

Response: _____

Psalm 138:3

Appeal: _____

Response: _____

> *Father, I stretch my hands to Thee, no other help I know.*
> *If Thou withdraw Thyself from me, O wherever shall I go?*
> AUTHOR UNKNOWN

Closing Thoughts

May the Lord teach us the need of fervent and importunate prayer! If we would follow the examples of the mighty Elijah or the distressed woman in Matthew, then we must pray boldly

> But I am poor and needy; yet the Lord thinketh upon me: thou art my help and my deliverer; Make no tarrying, O my God.
> Psalm 40:17

and not be discouraged by delayed answers. It is our nature to cast away our confidence in God (Hebrews 10:35). We are also very prone to fainting fits, as we will discover in our next lesson. But, if we would obey God's instructions for the practice of prayer, we will remember that we must

pray with faith.

pray with fervency.

For Our Children

FATHER, hear us, we are praying,
Hear the words our hearts are saying,
We are praying for our children.

Keep them from the powers of evil,
From the secret, hidden peril,
From the whirlpool that would suck them,
From the treacherous quicksand, pluck them.

From the worldling's hollow gladness,
From the sting of faithless sadness,
Holy Father, save our children.

Through life's troubled waters steer them.
Through life's bitter battles cheer them,
Father, Father, be Thou near them.

. . .

And wherever they may bide,
Lead them home at eventide.[5]

AMY CARMICHAEL

REV. EDWARD M. BOUNDS—THE PRAYING METHODIST

Like Praying John Hyde, E. M. Bounds (l835–1913) was of midwestern descent. Born in Missouri, he is best known for his ministry of prayer. Countless believers have profited from the eight very fine books he wrote on the subject.

E. M. Bounds was a chaplain for the Missouri troops during the Civil War. Twice he was a prisoner of war. He pastored several Methodist Episcopal churches in Missouri, Alabama, and Georgia. His final nineteen years of life were spent in Washington, Georgia.

During these fruitful years he gave himself more than ever to intercessory prayer. It was at this time that he authored several books challenging others in the matter of their prayer life. He also conducted itinerant revival meetings. One of his young preachers observed,

> *No man could have made more melting appeals for lost souls and back-slidden ministers than did Bounds. Tears ran down his face as he interceded for indolent preachers and people without Christ.*[6]

His ministry spanned four and a half decades, but this diminutive preacher never attracted a large personal following. Many admired him, and he was often asked to preach. He led many to the Lord over the years and profoundly touched many lives along the way. Someone has commented that few wanted to get too close to a man who pressed them to join a life of early morning prayer, humble service, and personal self-discipline. Sadly, that is still the case. Most of us would rather spend time serving instead of praying.

When E. M. Bounds wrote about the power of prayer, he wrote from personal experience. During his ministry years in Georgia, he would get up at 4:00 a.m. and pray until 7:00 a.m. As an elderly man he was still on his knees before the sun came up. How blessed were those individuals and ministries who knew their names were brought before the Lord daily by this dear saint of God. And how they must have missed him when he graduated to heaven one August morning in 1913. There were few, if any, other prayer warriors to take his place. Regrettably, that is still the case almost one hundred years later.

CHAPTER SEVEN
Prayer Practiced: Praying Without Fainting

"And he spake a parable unto them to this end, that men ought always to pray, and not to faint." (Luke 18:1)

In Luke 18 we find Jesus in the middle of a teaching session with His disciples. He follows the statement in verse 1 with a story of a woman who did not faint. He ends the story with a promise to answer the prayer of those who refuse to faint when they ask.

In our previous two lessons we have studied the actual practice of prayer. We've seen the importance of praying with faith and praying with fervency. Today's theme of prayer without fainting is equally important. What are the causes of fainting? What confidence does the Scripture give for potential fainters? What are the cures for fainting? All of these are important questions for those who would make prayer a priority in their lives, so let's get started on this very needed lesson!

The Causes of Fainting

Have you ever had a spiritual fainting fit? (Perhaps you are in the midst of one right now.) Let's start with a very basic question: What did Jesus mean when He commanded us not to faint? What is your definition of spiritual fainting?

Cause 1: Failure to Know and Believe the Promises of God[1]

1. Read Matthew 9:27–29. What simple question does Jesus ask here, and what simple answer was given by the blind men? _____

   _____

   _____

2. According to Matthew 13:53–58, why does God fail to do mighty works for us? _____

   Who were the people Jesus was speaking to in these verses?

   _____

Notice that they had personally heard His wisdom and freely acknowledged that He had done mighty works, but their hearts still would not believe Him.

3. In Acts 27:21–25, 44, what statement of faith does Paul make to the crew members of the storm-tossed ship?_____

   _____

   How is his statement similar to that of the men in Matthew 9?

   _____

Paul had received a promise from God, and by faith he believed the promise. God then wonderfully rewarded his faith with a great answer to prayer. Unlike believers in Bible times, we can hold all of His words in our hands. Why then do we not make acquaintance with His promises? We are sure to faint if we don't cling to the precious promises of God!

Cause 2: Failure to Willingly Submit to His Will

4. Read Jonah 4:8. Jonah is angry at God for sparing the repentant people of Nineveh. In this verse we read that the angry prophet had a fainting fit. What does he ask of God? _____

Jonah is like a little child pouting and demanding his own way, isn't he? He will not say, "Thy will be done," but insists that his will is most important. Do you know any believers who, by their similar attitudes, could be descendants of Jonah?

5. After reading Psalm 40:8, compare David's submissive spirit to that of Jonah. What is David's comment about doing God's will? _____

   _____

   Is this your testimony?_____

It is easy to sing about surrendering our wills and our hearts to Jesus, but we all know it is quite another thing to actually do what we sing! When, like Jonah, a believer engages in a continual struggle regarding submission to God, she will often end up in a fainting fit. A great missionary of the past often said that it is only by submitting to His will that we will ever find peace. A peaceful and quiet heart is one that is trusting God. Such a heart finds doing the will of God to be a delight and finds deliverance from fainting fits.

> *Take my will, and make it Thine;*
> *It shall be no longer mine.*
> *Take my heart, it is Thine own;*
> *It shall be Thy royal throne.*
> *It shall be Thy royal throne.*
> FRANCES HAVERGAL

Cause 3: Failures from Unknown Infirmities

6. Various physical conditions may lead a believer into bouts of depression or despondency. We women often don't know why we become so down-hearted and discouraged. Like the fainting psalmist in Psalm 42:5, 11, we may ask ourselves the same questions he asked. Write out the two questions he asked. _____

7. In times of discouragement we must find our hope where the psalmist found his. According to the second part of verses 5 and 11, where was that, and what expression of faith does he make here? _____

8. This godly man had great confidence in his faithful God. What words of assurance does he give us in verse 8?_____

> Meditating on God's faithfulness "will take your mind off the present situation and give hope that it will improve. It focuses your thoughts on God's ability to help you rather than your inability to help yourself. When you feel depressed, take advantage of this psalm's antidepressant. Read the Bible's accounts of God's goodness, and meditate on them."[2]

Cause 4: Neglect of Prayer

9. In Luke 18:1, Jesus gives an antidote for fainting. What is it?

_____

Spending time with God is a cure for fainting fits! Time spent in His presence waiting for help and direction will bring renewed strength. Isn't this the great truth given to us in Isaiah 40:31?

> *You surely cannot truly know the power of . . . God if you are able to live without prayer; for just as a man who is unable to breathe soon faints, so must a person spiritually faint if he does not pray.*[3]
>
> CHARLES SPURGEON

The Cures for Fainters

Two Old Testament saints testified of certain cures for believers who faint. Both give us fresh hope, and we find their encouraging words in the following Scriptures.

10. The slayer of Goliath gives a testimonial in Psalm 27:13–14. When David was about to faint, what gave him new strength? _____

_____

_____

11. Many years after David lived, the great prophet Isaiah prescribed a similar cure for fainting. God instructed him to write that strength to cure fainting fits comes from doing what? See Isaiah 40:31.

_____

What does it mean to wait upon the Lord? Does it include prayer?

_____

_____

> *Waiting on God is not easy. Often it seems that He isn't answering our prayers or doesn't understand the urgency of our situation. That kind of thinking implies that God is not in control or is not fair. But God is worth waiting for . . . because often God uses waiting to refresh, renew, and teach us.*[4]

The Confidence for Fainters

Let's end our lesson by returning to Isaiah 40. There are two great truths here that we need to ask God to write on our hearts. Confidence in the faithful God, Who directed Isaiah to write these words, has kept believers of many centuries from the perilous paths that lead to fainting.

Confidence 1: He Cannot Faint!

12. How does Isaiah describe our great God in Isaiah 40:28? _____

_____

_____

_____

13. Isaiah asks two questions before he describes the everlasting God. Write out the questions. _____

_____

_____

Why do you think he asked these questions of God's people? Surely believers have heard and know these truths about their God. But we often forget that our God is not like us. *He does not faint.* He does not become weary. He never lacks understanding or wisdom. But read on. Isaiah has even more good news for believers!

Confidence 2: He Strengthens Fainters!

14. According to verse 29, what two needful things does God promise to give to His fainting children?

He gives _____ to the fainting ones.

He gives increasing _____ to weak ones.

Notice how tenderly the Lord deals with His fainting people. He does not desert them or cast them off as being of no good to Him. He does what no one else can do for them when He gives them His sufficient power and deliverance.

> *May Thy rich grace impart*
> *Strength to my fainting heart,*
> *My zeal inspire;*
> *As Thou hast died for me,*
> *O may my love to Thee,*
> *Pure, warm and changeless be,*
> *A living fire!*
> RAY PALMER

Closing Thoughts

Isaiah tells us that "even the youths shall faint and be weary, and the young men shall utterly fall" (40:30). Yes, even the strongest of God's people can become weary and faint. Even the greatest of Bible men sometimes found themselves sitting under juniper trees telling

> *I had fainted, **unless** I had believed to see the goodness of the Lord in the land of the living.*
> *Psalm 27:13*

God they had no purpose for going on. We all know about juniper trees, don't we? I hope this lesson will help prepare our hearts for days ahead when we, too, feel no strength to walk on the paths He has chosen for us.

I have turned to Psalm 27:13 countless times when I was on the verge of yet another fainting fit. Let's revisit this verse as we end our lesson. May it bring encouragement to your fainting heart also.

JOHN BUNYAN—THE PRAYING PILGRIM

John Bunyan (1628–88) was a mender of pots and pans near Bedford, England, until he gave his wicked heart to Jesus at age twenty-five. The remaining thirty-five years of his life were spent mending the hearts of men and women who were broken because of sin.

Thanks to the printed page, this great man's numerous writings are still being used to bring men to Christ and to strengthen those who desire to walk closer to Christ on their pilgrim journey. Of course, one of Bunyan's books is, next to the Bible, one of the most published and purchased book of all times. More than three hundred years after its first publication, it is just as fresh and helpful as ever to present-day readers. *The Pilgrim's Progress* is so packed with Bible truth that, like the Bible, it can never be outdated.

Bunyan's own pilgrim journey to the Celestial City was often a discouraging one. Imprisoned for twelve years because he would not quit preaching salvation by grace alone, he and his family suffered greatly. A reading of his biography reveals, however, that he was not often given to fainting fits. His heart was fixed, trusting his God, and he used his many days in the Bedford Jail as a fruitful pulpit to preach, pray, and write. One of the books he wrote during this time was on the subject of prayer. Another was *The Pilgrim's Progress*.

Finally freed from his wrongful imprisonment, he continued to serve God as a faithful pastor and author. In his writings he often spoke of prayer. His words about this important topic can encourage us in our prayer life:

Pray often; for prayer is a shield to the soul, a sacrifice to God, and a scourge for Satan.""When thou prayest, rather let thy heart be without words, than thy words without a heart.[5]

John Bunyan has been with Christ for over three hundred years, but we give thanks that the fruit of his ministry, in the form of helpful books, still remains to help us grow and avoid the By-Path Meadows, Doubting Castles, and Vanity Fairs that continually surround us today.

CHAPTER EIGHT

Prayer Portraits: The Early Church

"They lifted up their voice to God with one accord." (Acts 4:24)

Having spent several lessons studying the principles and practice of prayer, we want to end this series with several encouraging prayer portraits from the Scriptures. Many in the Bible are known for their prayer ministries. Who could forget faithful Daniel and his three friends as they stood alone for God in a heathen land? Or, what about Elijah, Elisha, or Nehemiah? These are all examples of those who spent much time in communion with God, and He has put their prayer example in the Bible for our learning.

This study will allow us to look at only five prayer portraits: the early church, and God's servants Moses, Paul, Daniel, and David. These are great representatives of Bible men and women who prayed.

Today we travel back in time to the Upper Room, where Jesus had observed the Lord's Supper with His disciples before going to do His Father's will. We will see that the apostles, who assembled after Jesus' return to heaven, are different men from those who broke bread earlier with their Master. One of the great differences is the priority that prayer played in their lives.

Great Prayer at a Great Gathering

1. Read Acts 1:12–15. The church came into existence in a prayer meeting. Where was the meeting held, and how many were present? _____

2. What women were present at this meeting? _____

_____

In these verses we have the last mention of Jesus' mother, Mary. There is no mention of anyone worshiping her or praying to her.

3. According to verse 14, what type of spirit prevailed among them? (This was not always the case with the disciples, was it?)_____

_____

4. Acts 1:15–26 records the minutes of the very first church business meeting! What business did the church consider, and what prayer did they bring before the Lord?_____

_____

_____

   Why is prayer vitally important in the selection of spiritual leaders?

_____

_____

5. The men meeting in Jerusalem had once made a special request of Jesus. Read Luke 11:1, and record their request. _____

_____

   How do these verses in Acts show us that they had profited from time spent in Christ's school of prayer?_____

_____

The students graduated successfully it would seem. The priority of prayer in Jesus' life had now become their own. Those who had once looked to the Savior as their example were now examples themselves.

Great Prayer and Great Miracles

6. After reading the following passages, write down the wonderful works and miracles that happened because "prayer was made without ceasing of the church unto God" (Acts 12:5).

   Acts 2:37, 41 _____

_____

   Acts 2:43–47_____

_____

Acts 3:1–10 _____

_____

Acts 8:5–8 _____

_____

Acts 9:4–6 _____

_____

> As soon as Satan heard of the conversion of Saul,
> he ordered the devils into deep mourning!
> JOHN RYLAND

Acts 9:36–42 _____

_____

Acts 12:5, 12–17 _____

_____

What great things might be done in Bible-preaching churches today if all church members would continue steadfast in prayer? Think how our missionaries would have renewed strength to witness and work as never before! *There is a great price to be paid when the prayer closets of believers are neglected.* May the mighty works that happened through the labors of early believers make us hunger to see similar power in our own lives and churches.

> The angel fetched Peter out
> of prison, but it was prayer
> that fetched the angel![1]
> CHARLES SPURGEON

Great Prayer and Great Tribulation

7. Read about the first persecution in Acts 4. According to verses 2–4, what was the persecution, and why did it come about?_____

_____

_____

_____

What important thing did these wicked men notice about Peter and John?

_____

_____

What joyful happenings are recorded in verses 23–32?_____

_____

_____

_____

> *Notice how the believers prayed. First they praised God; then they told God their specific problem and asked for His help. They did not ask God to remove the problem, but to help them deal with it. This is a model for us to follow when we pray.*[2]

8. Read about the first martyr in Acts 6:8–15; 7:54–60. Name this early martyr and describe his spiritual life and work for God._____

_____

How does the Bible describe this powerful preacher's face (verse 15)?

_____

According to verses 9–12, why was he persecuted? _____

_____

Describe the crowd's response to Stephen's message, and Stephen's response to the crowd (verses 54–60). _____

_____

_____

_____

What was Stephen doing in the midst of the stoning (verse 59)?

_____

His prayer reached the ears of what very religious man (verse 58)?

_____

> *In testifying later, surely Paul must have thought in his heart that it was the prayer of Stephen that was the means of changing Saul the persecutor into Paul the Apostle.*[3]

9. Read about the second martyr in Acts 12:1–2. What apostle now gives his life for the sake of the gospel? _____

How did God deal with his murderer (12:20–23)? _____

10. Read about joy in a jail in Acts 16:16–34. In this story, one of Stephen's persecutors became the persecuted. Who was he and who was his companion? _____

   Whom did the Devil send to interrupt Paul's prayer meeting (verse 16)?

   _____

   For preaching Christ, these preachers received what punishment (verses 22–24)? _____

   _____

   What was Paul and Silas's response to these tribulations (verse 25)?

   _____

   _____

   Through prayer, what was accomplished in Philippi (verses 26, 33–34)?

   _____

   _____

11. The persecutions in Acts were a fulfillment of prophecy. Read John 15:20–21 and 16:1–4. What warning had Christ often given His disciples? _____

   _____

Great Prayer for Power to Serve

12. In Acts 6:2–4, what great works did the apostles devote themselves to?

   _____

   What work is listed first? _____

   As leaders in God's work, why was it more important for them to spend time with God rather than serving tables (verse 2)? _____

   _____

These early leaders had right priorities. Pioneer missionary Amy Carmichael also expressed this priority when she said, *"The work we do for God is not more important than the time we spend with God."* It is very easy to lose sight of this great truth when we are so busy serving God. Like Martha (Luke 10:38–42), our priorities are out of order and the Lord reminds us that busywork is not the most important work a Christian is to do.

13. Before sending Paul and Barnabas as missionaries, what did the believers do (Acts 13:1–3)? _____

_____

Do you think the church at Antioch sent these men on their missionary journey without prayer support? Why is prayer support equally as important as our financial support? _____

_____

What plan do you have to pray regularly for men and women who are supported by your church?_____

_____

Closing Thoughts

Prayer was a great priority with the men and women in the book of Acts. God was careful to record their emphasis on this vital subject so that we would have patterns to follow. I trust that this lesson will remind us once again of these patterns and that the Holy Spirit will impress on us that we must give ourselves to pray if we would have a ministry that will count for eternity. *"Lord, teach me to pray"* (Luke 11:1).

JAMES HUDSON TAYLOR—THE PRAYING MISSIONARY

James Hudson Taylor (1832–1905) was blessed with praying parents. His mother prayed fervently for his salvation, but it was not until he was seventeen that he gave his heart to Jesus Christ.

Soon afterwards he began training himself for missionary work in China. He believed God had called him to service in that needy land, and he gladly surrendered the comforts surrounding him in England to bring the life-changing good news of the gospel to idol worshipers in China. He began his preparation by studying medicine and languages. He especially worked at strengthening his faith. He knew he would not trust God in China if he did not trust Him in London. He began to practice a great truth that would become the theme of his ministry: *It is possible to move the hearts of men through God, by prayer alone.* This was a ministry conviction also shared by his contemporaries George Mueller and Amy Carmichael.

Hudson Taylor also firmly believed that "God's work, done in God's way, will never lack God's supply." This was another guiding principle in his life, and he proved its truth over and over while leading the ministry of China

Inland Mission. He was also heard to often testify, "I am the little servant of a great God." Our Lord is still looking for little servants who will, through prayer, expect great things from their great God.

> *How he trusted God for finances, not only for himself but also for others. How he was miraculously spared after being infected in the dissecting room, and how he grew in his exercise of faith are all told in his biographies. [As you read of his godly life,] you feel as if you are revisiting the book of Acts![4]*
>
> WARREN W. WIERSBE

Before he died, he had seen God supply every need for the work in China. Over one thousand men and women went to China as direct answers to his fervent prayers. His life of faith was their example, and they went forward all over China on their knees.

One of Taylor's close friends once wrote, "Oh, Hudson Taylor's life was surely a life worth looking into!" I encourage you to do just that. As you read, you will learn just what God can still do with those willing to give themselves wholly to prayer.

CHAPTER NINE

Prayer Portraits: The Prophet Moses

"And there arose not a prophet since in Israel like unto Moses, whom the Lord knew face to face." (Deuteronomy 34:10)

For this second prayer portrait we turn to the early books of the Old Testament. Throughout Exodus, Numbers, and Deuteronomy we find the following two statements many times: *"Moses spake unto the Lord"* and *"The Lord spake unto Moses."* For most of Moses' 120 years, this was the privileged relationship he enjoyed with God. After his death God wrote a great epithet for His friend. It is this epithet that begins this lesson.

1. Read Deuteronomy 34:10. What words did God write in the first part of this verse about His servant Moses? _____

   _____

2. In this same verse we read that "the Lord knew [Moses] _____ to _____." How is their relationship also described in the following verses?

   Exodus 33:11 _____

   Numbers 12:8 _____

3. Find the description of Moses' face in Exodus 34:29–35. How does the Bible describe him, who spent so much time in God's presence?

   _____

   _____

> *I am afraid that God could not afford to make our faces shine: we would grow too proud. We only read of two men whose faces shone, and both were very meek. The light on the face of Moses was the result of fellowship with God. May God the Holy Spirit cause our faces to shine today as we read of the shining face of Moses![1]*
>
> CHARLES SPURGEON

Face to Face—His First Forty Years

Moses' entire life was greatly influenced by his infant years. Any child born into a home with praying parents is a blessed child! (May all of our children be so born.) Moses' Levite parents have no recorded prayers in the Bible, but can we doubt that they continually sought God's face regarding their children? God pronounced these parents to be faithful, and He directed that they be included in His hero chapter, Hebrews 11.

4. Read Hebrews 11:23. By faith, what did Moses' parents do?_____

_____

5. Why do you think they were not afraid of the pharaoh's commandments?

_____

_____

In later years, who else was not afraid of Pharaoh (11:27)?

_____

6. Without God's help, no parents could have prepared Moses to make the choices he did as a young man. According to Hebrews 11:24–27, what important choices did he make? We should pray that our children will make similar decisions. _____

_____

_____

Moses' godly choices were stepping stones to a great ministry of fellowship with God and the leadership of His people. But at this point Moses was not ready to lead anyone. He would first need more preparation at Backside Desert University, where the student body consisted of only one student—Moses.

Face to Face—His Second Forty Years

7. According to Exodus 3:1, where was God's forty-year training school located? _____

   Moses worked his way through Backside Desert University. What was his job while a student? How did his surroundings here compare with the surroundings in which he had previously studied under Pharaoh? _____

   _____

8. While alone with God in the desert, he had plenty of time to meet with his Instructor. What did God teach him? Read Psalm 103:7 and write out the answer._____

9. Every Christian who desires to be used of God must grasp truths similar to those taught to Moses. Perhaps these truths are summed up best in Proverbs 3:5–7. List them below.

   a._____

   b._____

   c._____

   d._____

   e._____

   f._____

   g._____

10. Turn again to Exodus 3. Recorded here is one of the class sessions student Moses had with his Instructor. Read verses 10–13, and then write below if you think Moses was passing or failing. Does this session indicate that he had learned to trust God? _____

11. After many years of instructions, promises, and demonstrations from his Instructor, Moses was finally ready to graduate. Read Exodus 4:19–20. What did "the Lord say unto Moses" at the graduation? What was his response?_____

   _____

   _____

Could Moses have ever imagined the events of the forty years that lay before him? He would see with his eyes some of God's greatest miracles. He would hear with his ears the mighty voice of God. He would use his lips continually to fellowship and intercede with his wonderful God. The first eighty years of his life had indeed been almost indescribable, but they were nothing compared to the forty years now before him.

Face to Face—His Last Forty Years

Most of Moses' final forty were spent leading and interceding for God's rebellious people. In the next several passages we will see that our God is very longsuffering, merciful, and faithful, both to the rebels and to His servant Moses.

Murmuring was Israel's favorite pastime! It is also a great sin, not a mere weakness. In the following portions of Scripture we see how Moses and God dealt with Israel's continual whining.

12. Read Exodus 15:23–27. What was Israel's complaint? _____

_____

How did Moses respond? _____

_____

How did God respond to their unbelief? _____

_____

13. Read Exodus 16:2–9. What was Israel's complaint and blatant charge against God? _____

In verses 7–9, how did Moses respond? _____

_____

What was God's faithful response in verses 4–5? _____

_____

> *I must tell Jesus all of my trials;*
> *I cannot bear these burdens alone;*
> *In my distress He kindly will help me;*
> *He ever loves and cares for His own.*
> ELISHA A. HOFFMAN

14. Read Numbers 12:1–13. Who were the complainers in these verses, and what was their complaint? _____

_____

The little sister who had so lovingly watched over Moses' basket bed now rose up in rebellion against him. How this must have grieved him!

How did God respond to Miriam and Aaron's jealous remarks?

_____

How did the meek man Moses respond? _____

_____

Similar patterns of rebellion were repeated over and over during the forty years Moses led the children of Israel. ("Children" is a good way to describe them, isn't it?) But does it not remind us of our own sin pattern? Thankfully we have One Who is greater than Moses to intercede on our behalf (Hebrews 7:25).

15. Read Numbers 20:11–12. How did Moses sin against God?

_____

What punishment did God pronounce against him? Why would God punish His servant for something that seemed so insignificant?

_____

_____

Read Deuteronomy 3:23–29. What did Moses beg God to let him do?

_____

> In our age of lowering moral standards, we find it almost impossible to believe that God would punish Moses for the one time he disobeyed outright. What we fail to see, however, is that God did not reject Moses: Moses simply disqualified himself to enter the Promised Land. Personal greatness does not make a person immune to error or its consequences.[2]

God gave His response in verse 26. What was it? However, He would allow Moses to do what (see Deuteronomy 34:1–5 also)?_____

_____

Closing Thoughts

We never read that Moses complained about God's punishment. God's denial was not what he desired, but he accepted it as being best. He did not quit or get angry at God. His heart response was "Thy will be done," and he went about serving God and His people until his death. And then, no one came to his funeral! No, God allowed no one but Himself to lovingly conduct Moses' private burial. What an act of great lovingkindness God showed toward this one who had spent so much time in prayer and communion while walking on this earth.

We thank God for His servant Moses! His prayer portrait is indeed a valuable pattern for all of us who are called to be servants in this present century.

Dwight L. Moody—The Praying Evangelist

Unlike several of the great Christians we have written of in this study, Dwight Lyman Moody (1837–99) did not have praying parents. He was always thrilled to say that his mother was saved at one of his evangelistic meetings when she was seventy years of age. As a young boy, Moody was quite ignorant of the Bible and spiritual things, and he had little education of any sort.

In his late teens when Moody was living with an uncle in Boston, God brought into his life a godly Sunday school teacher named Edward Kimball. Mr. Kimball became concerned for Moody's soul and prayed earnestly for almost a year that this young man would be saved.

God answered his faithful prayers, and he led Moody to the Lord in the store where Moody was working as a shoe salesman.

This incident reminds us that we may be some young person's only intercessor. What a difference we can make by praying earnestly for those God places in our lives. What a difference Mr. Kimball made because of his interest in young Moody. We rarely hear any more about Edward Kimball, but for over one hundred years, believers have been talking about this great New England evangelist.

D. L. Moody labored for God as a children's Sunday school teacher in Chicago and later as a pastor and the founder of a Bible institute. Through his worldwide revival meetings thousands were brought to salvation in Christ.

One of Moody's best friends was the well-known Bible teacher Dr. R. A. Torrey. He once spoke of the reason God blessed Moody's ministries in such an unusual way. Torrey said, "I wish to testify that he was a far greater prayer than he was preacher. Time and time again he was confronted by obstacles that seemed insurmountable, but he always knew the way to overcome all difficulties was to pray, because nothing was too hard for His Lord."[3]

Let's return to Edward Kimball as we close. Would there have been a D. L. Moody if God had not brought a humble Sunday school teacher into his life? Is there a young person in our life for whom we can give ourselves to faithfully pray? Will we start a Kimball Prayer Circle? Yes, our country needs another D. L. Moody, but our young people greatly need more Edward Kimballs!

CHAPTER TEN
Prayer Portraits: The Prophet Daniel

"He kneeled upon his knees three times a day, and prayed, and gave thanks before his God." (Daniel 6:10)

A series on prayer is not complete without a careful look into the life of Daniel. What Sunday school child has not heard of this great man who peacefully spent a night with hungry lions because he would not stop spending time with his God in prayer? We can all learn much about prayer by looking carefully at the figure of this Jewish giant kneeling in prayer beside his window in the middle of Babylon.

In the plan of God, Daniel and hundreds of other teenage Jewish boys were taken as captives from Jerusalem to the heathen city of Babylon. Only God knew that Daniel would never again see his beloved Jerusalem because he would die an old man in Babylon. But he would not die before living over seventy years as personal counselor and advisor to four heathen kings and revealing to us the course of world governments from his time to the end of all time.

Someone has said that Daniel was an uncommon man in every way. He and godly Joseph are the only two Bible men about which there are no griefs, scandals, or disappointments revealed. It will profit us all to stand once again in the shadow of this Bible giant.

Daniel's Diligence

Why was Daniel so greatly beloved in heaven and on earth (Daniel 10:19)? Why have countless generations of believers studied his life and found him to be a worthy pattern of godliness? The answer to these questions are found in the first six chapters of the book that bears his name.

1. Only four of the hundreds of Jewish boys carried away into captivity are named for us. List some of the qualifications for those who were chosen and trained for royal palace service (Daniel 1:4). _____

   _____

   _____

   _____

   What "royal perks" did they receive (Daniel 1:5)? _____

   _____

2. Why do you think their Jewish names were changed to ones that honored Babylonian gods?_____

   _____

3. Why did Daniel and his friends purpose in their hearts (1:8) that they would not eat or drink any of the king's royal diet? Were they vegetarians?

   _____

   _____

> *Calvin says that when Daniel and his three friends got far enough away from the royal table they would gladly eat flesh with pleasant bread . . . in the wayside inns of Babylon, just as they had done at home in Jerusalem. It was the company at the king's table; it was the idolatry, the indecency, and indulgence that made Daniel determine that it would be both far easier and far safer to abstain altogether from the beginning.*[1]

How did God honor Daniel and his friends for their stand of godliness (1:10–20)?_____

_____

Daniel's Death Decree

King Nebuchadnezzar had a troubling dream, which he could not remember, and none of his "wise" men could reproduce the dream for him. A very furious king had a temper tantrum and decreed the death of all royal advisors, including Daniel and his friends. In a royal audience with the "furious" king, Daniel made an important announcement about the secret dream.

4. Prior to meeting with the king, he had a prayer meeting with his friends and declared he had a plan regarding the dream. What was the plan (2:14–18)? _____

_____

5. After God revealed the secret dream to Daniel (2:19), what words of praise did the faithful prophet give to God (2:20–23)?_____

_____

6. In revealing the dream, how did Daniel honor God (2:27–28)?

_____

How did King Nebuchadnezzar acknowledge God and honor Daniel (2:46–49)?_____

_____

_____

Daniel's Disclosures

We are bypassing the great story of God's holy champions in chapter 3 because we want to keep our emphasis on Daniel in this lesson. They, along with Daniel, were truly "example[s] of the believers" in every way. God has honored their faithfulness, and Daniel's, in Hebrews 11:33–34. But in Daniel 4 God tells us the story of the heathen king who came to faith in the true God because of the testimony of Daniel and his friends.

7. Astonished by the miraculous deliverance of Daniel's friends, the king used what words in 3:26–4:3 to praise God? _____

_____

_____

8. Chapter 4 tells of Nebuchadnezzar's fall from being the greatest king in the East to roaming in the fields and eating grass with animals! His kingdom had departed from him because of what sin (4:30)?

_____

_____

Later, in his right mind, what testimony to God's greatness and sovereignty did he give (4:34–37)? _____

_____

_____

How do 4:17 and 25 also declare that God is in charge of leadership for all nations? While ungodly men would scoff at the truth revealed here, why is it comforting to God's people?_____

_____

> Interpreters of Daniel 4 are divided over the matter of Nebuchadnezzar's salvation. The king himself provides the evidence of his salvation: (1) he did submit to God, (2) he did reap the benefit of that submission—his kingdom, and (3) he did worship God alone in direct contrast to his earlier life. The empire of Nebuchadnezzar has long since crumbled into dust, but the truth that he discovered remains.[2]

While the saga in the palace was continuing, Daniel was continuing his prayer life three times a day. See him at his window on his knees with his face toward Jerusalem. Hear him as he cries out to God for his needs and the needs of his people. (Perhaps it was his faithful prayers for King Nebuchadnezzar that turned the monarch's eyes toward heaven.) But there are three more heathen kings for Daniel to influence. Chapter 5 introduces us to a relative of Nebuchadnezzar.

9. Read 5:1–4. How did Belshazzar blaspheme God during his great feast?

_____

What was God's sudden response (5:5)?_____

_____

What was the king's astonished response (5:6–9)?_____

_____

10. Daniel's testimony for righteousness was known throughout the palace. How did the queen describe his character and value in 5:10–12?

_____

_____

_____

11. After refusing any bribes from the wicked king, what bold and coura-
    geous message did Daniel disclose to Belshazzar (5:18–24)?

    _____

    _____

    _____

    Daniel could have been killed instantly for speaking such prophecies of
    doom before this proud-hearted man. But after Daniel disclosed the writ-
    ing on the wall, how did the humbled king reward the faithful messenger
    (5:29)? _____

    _____

    How did God bring Daniel's message to fulfillment (5:30)? Who was the
    new king that Daniel would now serve (5:31)?_____

    _____

Daniel's Deliverance

Praying Daniel is now over eighty years old, and he was again chosen to be
one of Darius's top three advisors. He quickly earned the trust and respect of
the new king. We see in this chapter that Daniel would soon have great influence for good in King Darius's life. As one Bible teacher says, "He not only had
seniority in this group, he had superiority."[3]

12. Unable to find anything in Daniel's personal life to criticize, the jealous
    men attacked him in what area of his life (6:4–5)?_____

    _____

13. These deceitful princes deceived Darius into making what new law (6:7)?

    _____

    _____

    How many days would Daniel have been deprived of his prayer time with
    God? To save your life, would you be willing to stop praying openly for
    just a few days? _____

14. How did Daniel respond to the new law (6:10)? _____

    _____

The prophet's prayer life must have been known to many in Babylon. These men knew when and where to find Daniel in prayer. "Lord, teach us to pray like Daniel!"

15. While brave Daniel peacefully slept with an angel and the lions, how did King Darius spend the night (6:18)?_____

_____

What testimony to God's faithfulness and power did Daniel give in 6:22?

_____

According to 6:23, why was there not even one lion scratch on him?

_____

16. Like Nebuchadnezzar, King Darius also came to know the true God through the faithful testimony of praying Daniel. What words of praise did Darius have for God in 6:26–27? _____

_____

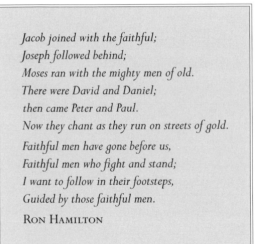

Jacob joined with the faithful;
Joseph followed behind;
Moses ran with the mighty men of old.
There were David and Daniel;
then came Peter and Paul.
Now they chant as they run on streets of gold.

Faithful men have gone before us,
Faithful men who fight and stand;
I want to follow in their footsteps,
Guided by those faithful men.

RON HAMILTON

There were fewer advisors in the palace after the events of chapter 6. Many of them were breakfast for hungry lions after Daniel climbed out of his supposed death den! The final verse of chapter 6 tells us that Daniel continued to prosper and pray as a royal advisor to Darius and his successor, Cyrus. He lived a fruitful life in every way, and he died in his old age in Babylon. Somewhere in the sands of present-day Iraq are the remains of this dear old man. But his powerful and prosperous life continues to convict all who will read the record God has given us of this great servant. We continue to be instructed by this one who "kneeled upon his knees three times a day and prayed and gave thanks before his God" (Daniel 6:10).

Closing Thoughts

Some of the most dramatic scenes in the Bible are found in the book of Daniel. How exciting to read of a thirty-foot golden idol, a fiery furnace, roaring lions, voices from heaven, an appearance by the mighty Gabriel, a lone finger writing a message on a wall, knees bowing to an idol, knees knocking in the royal palace, and praying knees in a west window pointed to far-off Jerusalem. It is this last scene of Daniel's praying that means the most to my heart. I have tried to visualize this faithful man on his knees three times a day seeking help from his God.

Thinking of his knees causes me to think of my own. How I wish there were calluses there because of countless hours in prayer. I'm afraid there are calluses on my feet from much service, but no calluses on my knees because of prayer. May God convict us about the condition of our knees! Wouldn't it be great if we had to have knee replacements because we prayed too much! "Lord, teach us to pray like Your beloved Daniel!"

GEORGE MUELLER—THE PRAYING FRIEND OF CHILDREN

After years of rejecting God, George Mueller (1805–98) was saved at the age of twenty in his homeland of Germany. Soon he moved to England to do missionary work, but God closed the door to foreign missions, and instead, opened to him one of the most unusual ministries ever conducted.

Mr. Mueller is a man all believers should be acquainted with. His testimony was like that of Caleb in Joshua 14:8: he wholly followed the Lord. God raised him up in the nineteenth century as a witness that He is indeed the hearer of prayer. Certainly we who must classify our own prayer lives as puny can learn much from this man Mueller, who was known by many as the "prayer pillar."

In 1836 God led him to begin his first orphanage in Bristol, England. From the beginning, he determined not to receive any fixed salary. He would depend fully on God's provisions. He also determined never to ask any person for financial help to support himself or his orphans but to make his needs known to God alone. Like his friend Hudson Taylor, he would ask only God to influence hearts to give to the work. He also purposed to owe no man anything and never to buy on credit.

Mr. Mueller never departed from these principles in the sixty-eight years he served God. He knew this was how God wanted him to conduct his ministry, but he never criticized other good brothers who built their ministries on other

Bible principles. Some did try to imitate him and, sadly, failed. He once commented, "I add here my solemn caution that none should act in this way for the sake of imitating me; otherwise he will learn to his bitter cost, what it is to do such things in the way of imitation."[4]

God used George Mueller to do a work that has seldom been equaled. During his day it was a striking testimony to the faithfulness of God, and it still is. Through prayer alone, he and his fellow laborers at the Wilson Street, and later the Ashley Down, orphanages saw the Lord send in provisions for every need of the thousands of children entrusted to his care. Children of all ages were housed, fed, clothed, and taught God's Word until they were able to support themselves in jobs for which they had been prayerfully trained.

Mr. Mueller did not pray just for funds for his Ashley Down ministries. He also prayed and gave to his friends such as Hudson Taylor and Charles Spurgeon. Taylor's China Inland Mission received over $15,000 from his friend Mueller, and he often sent gifts to help with the orphanage ministry Spurgeon founded. The great London preacher, in speaking of Mueller once commented, "I think sometimes that I would not mind changing places with George Mueller for time and eternity. I do not know anyone else of whom I would say so much."[5]

I encourage you to read more about George Mueller, the prayer pillar. While the reading of his life testimony will *inspire* your life, imitating his prayer habits will *change* your life.

CHAPTER ELEVEN

Prayer Portraits: The Apostle Paul

"I will therefore that men pray every where, lifting up holy hands, without wrath and doubting." (I Timothy 2:8)

Paul had been a praying man all of his life. As a Pharisee he continually said prayers, but these were spoken as mere rituals with the hope of gaining favor with God.

He prayed his first true prayer while on his knees on the road to Damascus. Speaking directly with Christ, he prayed perhaps the shortest prayer of his life, "Lord, what wilt thou have me to do?" (Acts 9:6).

I'm sure Paul never imagined how suddenly his life would change from being a chief Pharisee to being a chief apostle in the work of the risen Christ. But he did just that, and as we will see in this lesson, he gave himself wholly to his new Lord and Master.

In his many letters to new converts, he assured them of his prayers for them. He taught them the priority and practice of prayer, and he sought their prayer support for his labors.

We cannot look upon this great prayer portrait enough. From the life of this godly missionary we will learn some of our richest truths about the priority of prayer.

> *Prayer was so natural and so continual with the great Apostle that it found its way inevitably into his correspondence.*[1]
>
> J. Oswald Sanders

73

Paul: Perpetually at Prayer

From the day of his salvation until the day of his death, the Bible records for us the picture of Paul continually at the throne of grace.

1. Praying on Straight Street (Acts 9:10–20)—Whom does God send in Damascus to help Paul, a new believer?_____

   Why was Paul at the house of Judas on Straight Street?_____

   _____

   Why was Ananias somewhat reluctant to have a meeting with this man God called a "chosen vessel"?_____

   _____

   How did God use His servant Ananias to encourage His new servant Paul? _____

   _____

No one but our great God could have changed the heart of a fiery persecutor into one who immediately became a faithful pleader!

2. Praying in Antioch (Acts 13:1–3)—What specific requests are Paul and the saints at Antioch praying about? _____

   _____

3. Praying by the riverside (Acts 16:12–15)—In this great city, with whom did Paul and Silas have a prayer meeting? What woman is mentioned, and what work did God do in her heart? _____

   _____

4. Praying while locked in the stocks (Acts 16:23–33)—What time of night were these men having a prayer and praise service? _____

   _____

   What interrupted the praying and praising?_____
   In the wee hours of the morning, who was gloriously saved?

   _____

5. Praying in stormy weather (Acts 27:21–25)—In the middle of a great storm at sea, what heavenly messenger came to Paul, and what was his message?_____

   _____

   _____

How did Paul respond to this message?_____

In our stormy times, where are we to look for messages from God? What should be our response to these heavenly messages?_____

_____

_____

6. Praying while suffering (II Corinthians 12:7–10)—What was the burden on Paul's heart, and how many times did he pray about it? _____

_____

What was God's response to His troubled servant? _____

_____

What was Paul's response to his Master?_____

_____

Paul's Prayer List

Have you ever wondered what Paul's prayer list looked like? Did he have a very long scroll on which he carefully wrote down names, needs, and answers to prayer? (By the way, what does our prayer list look like?) While we cannot imagine the thousands of people Paul prayed for throughout his ministry, we do know who some of them were because Paul mentioned them in his letters.

Look up the following references; write down whom Paul was praying for and how often he prayed for them. (Only five examples are included here. There are many others.)

7. **Romans 1:7–9**

    Who?_____

    How often?_____

8. **Ephesians 1:1, 15–16**

    Who?_____

    How often?_____

9. **Philippians 1:1–4**

    Who?_____

    How often?_____

10. **II Timothy 1:1–3**

    Who?_____

How often?_____

11. **Philemon 1–4**

Who?_____

How often?_____

We can note from the above that Paul was praying for the saints, not to the saints!

Paul's Prayer Patterns

When Paul prayed for the saints, what did he ask God to do for them? We know from Scripture that he did more than ask God to bless them. The Scriptures record that he prayed for specific spiritual needs to be met in their lives. We do not see him praying for physical or material needs. Look up the following verses and record the specific requests you find. (Again, this is only a representative sample.)

12. In Ephesians 3:14–19 what did Paul ask God to grant and to do?

_____

_____

What did he pray they would be and know? _____

_____

_____

> One of the greatest tragedies of a believer's life is not unanswered prayer, but unoffered prayer.
> AUTHOR UNKNOWN

13. In each verse of Philippians 1:9–11 Paul had definite spiritual requests. What were they?_____

_____

_____

_____

14. Paul had never visited Colosse. How could he pray for people he had never met? Paul knew that the heart needs of every believer were the same

regardless of where they lived or how long they had been saved. Write his requests for these unseen friends below (Colossians 1:9–11).

_____

_____

_____

_____

_____

> *Too much of our prayer completely misses the mark. Listen to the prayer requests in an ordinary prayer meeting. You will note that with few exceptions the family of God is almost, if not altogether, earthly minded. The saints are burdened with the temporal and material and seem unaware of the greater spiritual needs.*[2]
>
> R. L. BRANDT

Paul's Prayer Requests

Yes, the chief of the apostles needed prayer! (As do all of us little disciples!) Godly man that he was, he knew that the great instruction Christ gave in John 15:5 included him. Write out this important verse:

_____

_____

_____

_____

Paul asked his fellow laborers to pray specific requests for him. Read the following verses and write down Paul's prayer requests.

15. **Romans 15:30–32**_____

_____

_____

At least three requests are found in the verses below. What are they?

16. **Ephesians 6:19** _____

_____

17. **Colossians 4:2–4** _____

_____

_____

18. **II Thessalonians 3:1–3** _____

_____

_____

_____

Closing Thoughts

Paul urgently sought the prayers of God's people. Did they pray? Only God knows, but could Paul have depended on us to pray for him? Who is depending on our prayers today? Are we remembering them before the throne?

> *"Most of us do not believe very strongly in prayer. We are very vocal on its importance, but we are very short on its performance. We would virtually defend our belief in it **with** our lives, but we do not practice it **in** our lives."*[3]

The above statement is very convicting, is it not? It describes many present-day believers. It would be alarming to know the true amount of time the average member of our Bible-preaching churches truly prays. And when we do pray, do we pray biblically? Do we pray for the spiritual needs of those on our prayer lists, or only for physical and material needs? Remember that the great apostle left us a pattern of praying for heart needs!

It is refreshing to look at prayer portraits of the early church, Moses, Daniel, and Paul, isn't it? The portraits of great saints need to be studied often as reminders of what God-honoring prayer warriors look like.

Do you know any believers who are true prayer warriors? Could you be classified as such a person?

DAVID BRAINERD—A PRAYING FRIEND OF NATIVE AMERICANS

In 1718 in the colony of Connecticut, there was born a man named David Brainerd. Before he would complete his short life on this earth in 1747, he would influence countless Native Americans for Christ. He would also reach around the world through his convicting journals and provide fuel for great ministries begun by Charles and John Wesley, Henry Martyn, George White-field, and William Carey, among others.

Although raised in a strict Puritan home, David rejected Christ until the age of twenty-one. Even at that young age he was beginning to show signs of the disease of tuberculosis, which afflicted him throughout his adult life. After a short time as a student at Yale College, he began to prepare himself for the ministry by studying with a Connecticut pastor near New Haven. It was during this time of preparation that he began to be burdened regarding a mission to the spiritually neglected Indian people.

Humanly speaking, David was not the man to reach these long-forgotten people. They were spread over a large area and roads were primitive. Travel was generally by horseback and David's health was very frail. There were no translated portions of the Scriptures, and the Indians were often hostile to the gospel. Many were also steeped in the tribal religious customs, and the white man had introduced them to deadly alcohol.

But none of these things moved David Brainerd. He began to pray and trust God to go before him and make the many "crooked places" straight (Isaiah 45:2). He believed God could make a way into the wilderness Indian villages of New Jersey, New York, and Pennsylvania. He began to pray. Before making contacts with the Indians, he spent entire days and nights before the throne of grace. This would be his pattern for the eight years of his ministry, and he would soon be known to many as "The Apostle of Prayer."

> David Brainerd did his greatest work by prayer. What was he praying for? He knew that he could not reach these souls; he did not understand their language. Therefore he knew that anything he might do must be absolutely dependent upon the power of God.[4]

Traveling through hundreds of miles of rugged country, he labored alone most of the time. He eventually established and pastored several Indian churches and saw a great number of his beloved Stockbridge, Delaware, and Susquehanna Indians saved and baptized.

By his late twenties the last stages of tuberculosis were upon him, and he could physically do no more. He returned to the Massachusetts home of his friend, the godly Puritan Jonathan Edwards. It was in the town of Northampton on October 9, 1747, that he died and was laid to rest in the town cemetery. His friend Jonathan Edwards conducted his funeral. His fiancée, Jerusha Edwards, would be buried beside him in four months.

David Brainerd had only eight years to serve God, but because of his fervent prayer life he was able to accomplish more than most men do in a lifetime. His journal is filled with reasons he is qualified to be called "The Apostle of Prayer." These simple writings of striving with God for the souls of men are still used to convict and stir men and women who also hunger to please God by coming boldly, and continually, before His throne of grace.

CHAPTER TWELVE

Prayer Portraits: King David

"Evening, and morning, and at noon, will I pray, and cry aloud: and he shall hear my voice." (Psalm 55:17)

We conclude our series on prayer by looking at the priority of prayer in the life of King David, the greatest king of Israel. Having looked at four great prayer portraits already, it should encourage our hearts to conclude with a portrait of the much-loved person known as the "man after God's own heart" (Acts 13:22).

David's heart is displayed on each page of the greatest prayer and praise book ever written, the book of Psalms. This lesson will take us on an encouraging journey through this inspiring book. Our travels will remind us of the many cries and prayers that arose from David's heart. We will also stop several times to hear David's wonderful words of confidence and praise to our mighty God.

1. How is David described in Acts 13:22? What do you think this means?

   _____

   _____

2. Read Psalm 78:70–72. What is the title given David in verse 70?

   _____

   What responsibility for service did God first give David? What greater responsibility did this lead to (78:71)? _____

   _____

According to 78:72, how well did David perform his jobs of leadership?

_____

David, faithful in little things, was blessed as God entrusted him with greater responsibility. As a shepherd boy he was faithful to pray and seek God's guidance.

As a powerful king he continued to acknowledge his need of God by seeking His face morning, noon, and night. One request that was often on his lips was for guidance. A godly man does not desire to follow the guidance of the world; his desire is only for heavenly counsel. Looking at some of David's prayers for guidance will assure us of two things: (1) We do not have enough wisdom to direct our own lives. (2) God will direct our steps today just as faithfully as He directed David's.

David Prays for Guidance

3. What two requests did David make in Psalm 5:8? David had some "crooked places" in his life that he wanted God to make plain to him. What "crooked places" are you dealing with today? Will you seek God's help in straightening them out, even as King David did?_____

   _____

   _____

4. Read Psalm 25:4–5. What four requests did the psalmist make here?

   _____

   _____

   According to verse 5, how much time did David say he spent waiting on God for direction? _____

5. According to Psalm 48:14, how long does God promise to be our faithful guide? Why should this truth bring comfort to our hearts? _____

   _____

6. Our heavenly guide has given us a great guide book for our journey here below. How does this guide book help us? See Psalm 119:105. _____

   _____

> We often pray for God's guidance as we struggle with decisions. What we need
> is both guidance and a guide—a map that gives us landmarks and directions
> and a constant companion who has an intimate knowledge of the way and will
> make sure we interpret the map correctly. The Bible will be such a map, and
> the Holy Spirit will be the constant companion and guide.[1]

7. Where is the first place you turn for guidance? The Scriptures? Friends? Other books? _____

What great promise is given for guidance-seekers in Psalm 32:8? This is a special verse of assurance to mark and memorize for days ahead!

_____

_____

David Prays in Adversity

Even mighty kings have problems! David's life, like ours, was often filled with trials and heartaches. In Psalm 132:1 he prayed this short and simple prayer: "Lord, remember David, and all [of] his afflictions." In several psalms he questioned God about his troubles, and often he wrote of crying unto God for relief from his sorrows. We thank our Lord for including the portrait of David's troubles in the Word. It is encouraging to know that even the "man after God's own heart" had heavy burdens and griefs to bear!

David's Questions for God

8. The psalmist had two questions for God in Psalm 10:1. Write them below.

_____

_____

What are some reasons that God may *seem* far from us?_____

_____

_____

The psalmist did not like the thought of God being far from him. According to Psalm 145:18, during another time in his life, he expressed the joy of knowing what truth?_____

_____

_____

9. In Psalm 13:1–2, David asked God four questions. What were they?

_____

_____

_____

David seemed to be somewhat "down in the royal dumps" at the time he wrote these words. Have you ever asked God similar questions? Write some of your questions below. _____

_____

_____

_____

David began this psalm with a lot of sighs, but how does he end it (13:5–6)?_____

_____

_____

What lesson(s) can we learn for ourselves from his "how long?" song?

_____

_____

10. What searching question does David ask in Psalm 119:82? _____

_____

_____

If a Christian friend asked you a similar question, how would you answer her? What comforting verses could you share with her? List several.

_____

_____

_____

David Cries to His God

11. David's eyes were toward the Lord in all areas of his life, but he especially ran to God in times of sorrow. In the psalms he used the expression of crying to His Lord over twenty-five times. Read the following verses and write down David's words about crying to God in times of distress.

Psalm 18:6 _____

_____

Psalm 34:6, 17 _____

_____

Psalm 119:145–147 _____

_____

Psalm 138:3 _____

_____

Psalm 142:5–7 _____

_____

David's Confidence in God

Like Abraham, another of God's friends, David was confident that what God had promised He was able to perform (Romans 4:21). May the following words from David's heart help to increase our confidence and faith.

12. Of what was David confident in Psalm 27:3, 5, 13–14? _____

_____

_____

13. After reading Psalm 34:17–19, 22, write down the great promises given here for the righteous. Then ask God to write them upon your heart, for they are too precious to be forgotten. _____

_____

_____

14. According to Psalm 119:75, what knowledge and confidence dwelt in David's heart?_____

_____

_____

What similar confidence did the apostle Paul express in Romans 8:28?

_____

_____

A WOMAN OF PRAYER

15. Note David's confidence in Psalm 138:7–8. Of what was he fully per-
    suaded?_____

    _____

How blessed to know that our God is concerned about all that concerns His
children. May David's words of confidence in God bring new assurance to our
own hearts!

David Praises His God

In spite of many griefs in his life, David was a man given to the praise of his
God. He continually gave to God the *"freewill offerings of his mouth"* (Psalm
119:108). May the following words from his mouth challenge our hearts to do
the same.

16. According to Psalm 34:1, how often are we to bless (praise) our Lord?

    _____

    What are some of the "all times" that might make it difficult to give
    praise? _____

    _____

    _____

> *We ought to talk of the Lord's goodness on pur-
> pose so that others may be confirmed in their
> trust in a faithful God.*[2]
> CHARLES SPURGEON

17. Some of David's greatest words of praise are found in Psalm 103. After
    reading through the psalm, write down those works and acts of God for
    which David gave praise. _____

    _____

    _____

    _____

    _____

> *We receive all of these without deserving any of them. No mat-*
> *ter how difficult your life's journey, you can always count your*
> *blessings—past, present, and future. When you feel as if you*
> *have nothing for which to praise God, read David's list!*[3]

Closing Thoughts

Learning to pray is a lifelong experience. None of us is satisfied with our prayer life. My prayer is that these lessons have made each of us even more dissatisfied! Who among us can say we spend enough time with God? May the sin of prayerlessness be to us truly sinful because *"the sin of prayerlessness is the cause of a powerless spiritual life!"*[4]

I used the following statement in our first lesson. It is from a small booklet written by a godly man who taught college students for many years. His book entitled *The Principles and Practice of Prayer* was helpful and convicting as I wrote these lessons. I think his concluding statement in the book is especially insightful,

> *Let Thy presence, blessed Savior,*
> *Our protection ever be;*
> *Give us strength for every trial,*
> *Keep, oh, keep us close to Thee.*
>
> *How we feel our burden lighter,*
> *Till we loose our weight of care,*
> *While we lift our hearts together*
> *In the simple, earnest prayer.*
> FANNY CROSBY

and I conclude with it with the hope that it will remind us all of the necessity of getting serious about the matter of prayer, and the importance of its priority in our lives.

> *"There is little value in talking about, studying and reading about prayer if we do not pray.* **In fact, learning about prayer can be positively harmful because it increases our responsibility and intensifies our guilt if we fail to pray.** *Prayer is one of the highest privileges of the child of God, the most significant form of service that can be rendered to God and men, and is the duty of every believer.* **Therefore, we must pray!**"[5]

Notes

Chapter 1

[1]Ivan H. French, *The Principles and Practice of Prayer* (Lincoln, NE: Back to the Bible, 1983), p. 112.

[2]Andrew Murray, *With Christ in the School of Prayer* (Old Tappan, NJ: Fleming H. Revell Co., 1953), p. 17.

[3]French, p. 110.

Chapter 2

[1]J. Oswald Sanders, *Spiritual Leadership* (Chicago: Moody Press, 1967), p. 110.

Chapter 3

[1]An Unknown Christian, *The Kneeling Christian* (Grand Rapids: Zondervan Publishing House, 1945), p. 118.

[2]*Life Application Study Bible*, (Wheaton, IL: Tyndale House Publishers, 1997), p. 1112.

[3]Tacy Bly, *Frances Ridley Havergal* (New Canaan, CT: Keats Publishing, 1977), p. 148.

Chapter 4

[1]Charles H. Spurgeon, *Twelve Sermons on Prayer* (Grand Rapids: Baker Book House, 1971), p. 8.

[2]Spurgeon, p. 11.

[3]Frank Houghton, *Amy Carmichael of Dohnavur* (Fort Washington, PA: Christian Literature Crusade, n.d.), p. 2.

[4]Herbert Lockyer, *All the Prayers of the Bible* (Grand Rapids: Zondervan Publishing House, 1959), p. 152.

[5]Rosalind Goforth, *How I Know God Answers Prayer* (Grand Rapids: Zondervan Publishing House, 1921), p. 5.

Chapter 5

[1]Lehman Strauss, *Sense and Nonsense About Prayer* (Chicago: Moody Press, 1974), p. 42.

[2]Tom Carter, *Spurgeon at His Best* (Grand Rapids: Baker Book House, 1988), p. 72

[3]Arthur W. Pink, *The Attributes of God* (Grand Rapids: Baker Book House, 1975), p. 52.

[4]Charles H. Spurgeon, "Introduction," *Prayers of Spurgeon* (Pasadena, TX, Pilgrim Publication, 1990).

[5]Spurgeon.

Chapter 6

[1]Lockyer, p. 75.

[2]*Life Application Study Bible*, p. 1595.

[3]Charles H. Spurgeon, *The Gospel of the Kingdom* (Pasadena, TX: Pilgrim Publications, 1974), p. 125.

[4]*Life Application Study Bible*, p. 2162.

[5]Amy Carmichael, *Toward Jerusalem* (Fort Washington, PA: Christian Literature Crusade, 1988), p. 106.

[6]Lyle W. Dorsett, *E. M. Bounds, Man of Prayer* (Grand Rapids: Zondervan Publishing House, 1991), p. 59.

Chapter 7

[1]Charles H. Spurgeon, *Spurgeon's Expository Encyclopedia,* Vol. 6 (Grand Rapids: Baker Book House, 1985), p. 405.

[2]*Life Application Study Bible*, p. 989.

[3]Spurgeon, p. 409.

[4]*Life Application Study Bible*, p. 975.

[5]I.D.E. Thomas, *A Puritan Golden Treasury* (Carlisle, PA: Banner of Truth Trust, 1977), p. 211.

Chapter 8

[1]Charles H. Spurgeon, *Only a Prayer Meeting* (Pasadena, TX: Pilgrim Publications, 1976) p. 11.

[2]*Life Application Study Bible*, p. 1880.

[3]Tom Carter, *Spurgeon at His Best* (Grand Rapids: Baker Book House, 1988), p. 311.

[4]Warren W. Wiersbe, *Walking with the Giants* (Grand Rapids, MI: Baker Book House, 1976), p. 63.

Chapter 9

[1]Charles Spurgeon, *Spurgeon's Expository Encyclopedia,* Vol. 11 (Grand Rapids: Baker Book House, 1985), pp. 168–69.

[2]*Life Application Study Bible*, p. 133.

[3]E. F. and L. Harvey, *Kneeling We Triumph* (Shoals, IN: Old Paths Tract Society, 1982), p. 15.

Chapter 10

[1]Alexander Whyte, *Bible Characters* (Grand Rapids: Zondervan Publishing House, 1967), p. 402.

[2]*Biblical Viewpoint, Focus on Daniel* (Greenville, SC: Bob Jones University, 1974), p. 125.

[3]J. Vernon McGee, *Thru the Bible with J. Vernon McGee,* Vol. III (Pasadena, CA: Thru the Bible Radio, 1982), p. 563.

[4]Charles H. Spurgeon, *The Sword and the Trowel* (Pasadena, TX: Pilgrim Publications, 1975), p. 17.

[5]Lewis Drummond, *Spurgeon—Prince of Preachers* (Grand Rapids: Kregel Publications, 1992), p. 420.

Chapter 11

[1]J. Oswald Sanders, *Prayer Power Unlimited* (Chicago: Moody Press, 1977), p. 53.

[2]R. L. Brandt, *Praying with Paul* (Grand Rapids: Baker Book House, 1966), p. 100.

[3]Brandt, p. 98.

[4]Oswald J. Smith, *David Brainerd—The Man of Prayer* (Grand Rapids: Zondervan Publishing House, 1939), p. 5.

Chapter 12

[1]*Life Application Study Bible*, p. 994.

[2]Charles H. Spurgeon, *The Treasury of David*, Vol. 1 (McLean, VA: MacDonald Publishing Company, n.d.), p. 123.

[3]*Life Application Study Bible*, p. 1037.

[4]Andrew Murray, *The Believer's Prayer Life* (Minneapolis: Bethany House Publishers, 1983), p. 21.

[5]French, p. 110.